ACING THE COLLEGE APPLICATION

ACING THE COLLEGE APPLICATION

How to Maximize
Your Chances
for Admission to the
College of Your
Choice

MICHELE A. HERNANDEZ, Ed.D.

Ballantine Books  New York

2007 Ballantine Books Trade Paperback Edition

Copyright © 2002, 2007 by Michele A. Hernández, Ed.D.

Published in the United States by Ballantine Books, an imprint
of The Random House Publishing Group, a division of Random
House, Inc., New York. Originally published in different form by
Ballantine Books, a division of Random House, Inc., in 2002.

BALLANTINE and colophon are registered trademarks
of Random House, Inc.

ISBN 978-0-345-49892-2

Printed in the United States of America

www.ballantinebooks.com

9 8 7 6 5 4 3 2 1

To my friends, my family,
and all the parents
who have allowed me to work
with their superstar children.
And to my loving husband, Bruce,
and my two adorable children,
Alexia and Ian.
Not to mention the
two furry family members,
Harris and Bree,
our golden retrievers.

# CONTENTS

Contents

Contents

INTRODUCTION

WHO NEEDS TO READ THIS BOOK?

If you are applying to colleges that fall into the selective or highly selective category, this book is for you. Even for those applying to less selective colleges, this book will still be of great help in filling out all parts of the application. For selective colleges, the application is what distinguishes one applicant from another. Thousands of colleges fall into the selective and highly selective categories, including almost all that are listed in the *U.S. News and World Report* annual college ranking issue: "America's Best Colleges."

Many schools have now moved to honor the Common Application, an application that is uniform for more than three hundred colleges. Therefore, essay questions for many schools follow a common pattern and are more predictable year to year. Even so, there are still many schools (the University of Chicago, Northwestern, MIT, Cornell, and the University of Michigan, to name a few) that take great care in developing unique essay questions that purposely don't overlap with questions from other schools' applications. This book will take you by the hand and lead you step-by-step through the application process, from visiting colleges and requesting applications to mailing in your applications to the colleges. It provides many actual examples from short answer questions to essays from students I've worked with over the years.

Why is the application so important? The simple answer is that there are so many academically strong students in the United States who apply to so many of the same schools that even schools that used to be considered safety schools are now much more selective. These so-called second-tier colleges are now very difficult to be accepted to as well. In 2007, Boudoin College accepted only 18 percent of its applicants and Middlebury College accepted only 23 percent, record lows. The admissions office will see thousands of students with strong standardized test scores, strong high school records, strong teacher recommendations, and good leadership positions. At a certain level, the only way to distinguish among students with excellent records is to judge the student on personal merit—that impression comes directly from the student's writing in the application. Thus, students cannot afford to assume that they will be accepted solely on their academic merits without putting the necessary time into the application process. Students who ignore the importance of self-presentation in the application do so at their peril.

Recently there has been a huge rise in the number of applications to top colleges. Comparing just the two-year period from 2004 to 2006, Harvard's applications jumped 15 percent, Yale's 7 percent, Princeton's 29 percent, Columbia's 9 percent, Brown's 20 percent, Dartmouth's 11 percent, Penn's 13 percent, and Cornell's a whopping 35 percent. In the face of such odds, this book will break the process down into smaller steps and take the tension and anxiety out of a process that students enjoy about as much as getting a tooth pulled.

Are you a bright, motivated student? If so, you are more likely than most to need help completing your college applications. Why? Because it is precisely the most intelligent, most creative, and most interesting students who have the hardest time packing themselves into the tight constraints of the college application. The fault lies with the whole idea of the college application. Colleges ask you to summarize everything important that you've done in your first seventeen years or so into just a few pages. Obviously, you have to know what admissions people are looking for to do a convincing job. The task can appear overwhelming, especially when you consider that many colleges still have their own specific applications rather than one common set of forms. Applying to ten to fifteen colleges can mean writing more than ten different essays just to cover the basic questions asked. To make matters worse, writing for the admissions office is nothing like writing a paper for your English teacher. Despite what most people think, admissions officers read the various parts of the application, including the main essay, mostly for content, not for writing style. Therefore, it is not worth it to struggle to write Faulknerian prose when plain old John Grisham will often do the trick.

 ## WHY YOU NEED AN INSIDER'S VIEW

You will get tons of solicited and unsolicited advice from teachers, guidance counselors, students, and alumni. Though they all will have good intentions, they all lack one qualification: They did not work in an admissions office. Why is this important? Only someone who has actually spent several years working in a college admissions office knows and understands the inner workings and nuances of the admissions process. High school guidance counselors know only what colleges *want* them to know about the process, as do students and parents. Admissions officers share only *select* information with the public, including guidance counselors, although they will share more specific information with the latter group. Though I don't want to spend time listing all the half-truths, myths, and misrepresentations perpetrated by admissions offices, I'll give one quick example of what I mean. You approach an admissions officer from a selective school and recount your mediocre test scores. You then ask if you should apply. Even if the admissions officer realizes that you have virtually no chance of admission, he or she is trained to encourage you to apply anyway. Why? First of all, admissions officers have an ungodly number of applications to wade through, so the worse an application is, the less time it takes to read it. Few will admit this basic truth, but it takes less than five minutes to read the application of a grossly under-qualified applicant. In addition, these weaker applicants usually require only one reading (hence the term "one-reader reject") and a quick perusal by the director, so the admissions staff gets a break. Second and most important, colleges are always on the lookout to improve their selectivity rating. That is to say that if more students apply and are subsequently rejected, a college can say it admitted only 20 percent of those who applied rather than a higher number such as 30 percent. Because parents and students are fixated by national rankings (by the likes of *U.S. News and World Report* and many college guides), they specifically look for schools with the lowest selectivity rates.

Unfortunately, students often rule out a college because it appears to be easy to get into. I say unfortunately because selectivity alone doesn't tell you much. Cornell's very competitive and nationally known school of engineering admits roughly 35–40 percent of its applicants, while the less competitive general school of arts and sciences admits roughly 25 percent. On the surface it looks as if the engineering school is easier to get into, but that is not the case—the pool of students willing to commit to this rigorous engineering program includes some of the best students in the country. A C student with a low math ability would never in his right mind apply to an engineering school, while he might send in an application to a liberal arts school. In other words, the pool is self-selective in the first place. The same phenomenon is evident at some of the top women's colleges, including Smith, Wellesley, and Bryn Mawr. I've worked with many students who rule out women's colleges because they assume from the selectivity index that they are less competitive—this is not true!

I worked in the Dartmouth admissions office in the nineties. Those who worked in these offices in the seventies and eighties faced a dramatically different admissions scene with very different admissions standards, even at the most selective colleges. Most guidance counselors don't know the whole behind-the-scenes admissions story. Admissions officers spend three months out of the year, every year, visiting four to five high schools a day, speaking to students and college counselors. Though there are some terrific counselors who really know what they are talking about, the majority are too overwhelmed by their job to be able to give the kind of personal assistance necessary to produce a first-rate application. At most public schools, counselors are responsible for anywhere from one hundred to five hundred students! That means they have to write at least a hundred letters of recommendation and fill out checklists, transcript requests, et cetera, for every single student. Plus, they schedule all the college visits. How can we expect this group to provide one-on-one advice?

At smaller private schools, there are lots of excellent and caring counselors, but there are just as many who never had a solid grasp of the current state of selective college admissions. I can recall counselors who would send ten applicants with subpar qualifications to Dartmouth and then wonder why not one was accepted. They have an almost impossible task: to keep track of all the changes in the admissions process, fill out all the paperwork, orient all the students and parents, and then read every student's application materials. It's not possible, which is why some parts of the job ultimately get compromised. And you guessed it—the part that gets compromised is the individual help to the students writing the applications. I see this firsthand in my current role as a college consultant because my clients come from some of the most prestigious private and public schools in the country, and even there, at our nation's best schools, counselors just don't have enough hours in the day to do more than proofread applications in a cursory fashion. When I work with a student and his or her family, we usually spend between fifty and one hundred hours of contact time from start to finish, completing applications.

One criticism of independent counselors is that students who work with them tend to come out looking too packaged. Packaging is not what the admissions process is all about. Any materials that are overly edited or have too much adult input come across as such in the process. Because parents tend to overedit, I recommend that students enlist a teacher or a guidance counselor's help in reading over essays.

It is imperative to preserve your own voice. The top independent counselors spend enough time with students to get to know their strengths, their hopes, their talents, their leadership abilities, their personalities, their hobbies, their pets, their favorite books and films, the kinds of magazines they read, and their favorite foods. You have to know a student well to be able to highlight the key aspects of his achievements to date. Many top admissions directors agree. In an August 2006 *Time* magazine cover story, "Who Needs Harvard," Lee Stetson, dean of admissions at the University of Pennsylvania, said about independent consultants, "Some of them are very helpful and are helping students learn how to tell us about themselves." Reading this book will help you pinpoint your most interesting features and learn how to highlight them for the admissions office. In effect, you will learn how to tell admissions officers more about what makes you special.

The fact that you have picked up this book shows that you care about the quality of your applications. The application is your best chance to tell your story. Make it memorable! You'll find that once you familiarize yourself with how your application is read by admissions officers, you will be better able to write essays that improve your chances of admission to the college of your choice. The more prepared you are, the stronger your applications. The one with the strongest application does win the prize, in this case a letter of admittance. I've tried to lay out the path in a logical fashion that will lead you step-by-step through the maze of fill-ing out college applications.

Beginning with the activity list, the chapters progress from the smaller essays to the main essays, and then to the specifics of every application. Once these distinct pieces are crafted, they will be plugged into the Common Application during the final steps. I've picked as examples some of my favorite essays and responses from my clients, which I hope will make this book entertaining as well as informative. Onward we go to the first part of the application: the activity list.

ACING THE COLLEGE APPLICATION

I

THE ACTIVITY LIST

I find it incredible that one of the most important components of the application is the one that many applicants don't bother with. Overall, colleges judge students roughly 60 to 80 percent on their academic record and 20 to 40 percent on their record of extracurricular accomplishments. Unfortunately, most school counselors don't know their students well enough to summarize a student's on-campus leadership (not to mention any off-campus leadership that they would not know about at all), so it just doesn't get mentioned. Students usually content themselves with the bare bones activity list required on the Common Application. The problem is that many activities are unusual or require additional explanation—it is simply impossible to fit any descriptive or explanatory notes into those tiny boxes on the provided grid. Granted, some activities and roles don't need much explanation, but what happens if you founded an organization to raise money for bone marrow transplants? Naturally, the admissions office would want to know how you became interested in your activity and what your role was in it. What happens if your most important activities (say, music, dance, art, or karate) are done completely out of school? How can you communicate your involvement to the admissions office? Enter, stage right, the activity list.

No matter what admissions officers tell you about the importance of leadership, keep in mind that academics are weighted more in the admissions process than extracurricular leadership. No matter how strong you are in leadership, you will still need at least a solid academic record for selective and highly selective schools. As a general rule, the less selective a college is, the more likely it is to give more weight to your extracurricular record. For the most selective schools, academics rule the day, with extras a distant second. To put it another way, strong academics open the door, while substantial talents may get you inside.

Given the bias toward academics, why is the activity list so important? Basically, it helps to differentiate between the thousands of generally strong students who apply to the top colleges. Between two solid students of roughly equal academic merit, doesn't it make sense that a master oboe player would be accepted over someone who has participated in only a few clubs or activities? For students who have become highly involved with their high school (or outside of their high school, as we will discuss shortly), the activity list is the place to showcase how their free time is spent.

Colleges want *high-impact* recruits. The college gets much more mileage out of a student who is either a sports star, a great musician, a campus activist, or a published writer than it does out of someone who goes back to the dorm after class and channel-surfs. You represent an investment for the college. Like any investor, colleges seek an aggressive return on their investment. Therefore, they look for students who are active, show leadership, and have demonstrable skills in a specific area such as sports or music—in short, those who will make a difference, those who will be remembered years later. That's why colleges also like a few celebrities if they can attract them because their mere presence brings positive press to the college. We all know that Chelsea Clinton chose Stanford and Amy Carter chose Brown and both schools have benefited tremendously from the association with presidents. Brooke Shields's tenure at Princeton probably did more for Princeton's endowment and academic ranking than all other efforts combined.

 ## INITIATIVE AND PASSION

Colleges look for students who show *initiative* and *passion*. These are the two mantras you should repeat to yourself over and over as you fill out your applications. Initiative in the context of the college application means going beyond basic requirements to achieve something of note. For example, let's take a student who loves studying languages. Unfortunately, his private school has very limited language courses, offering only Spanish, Latin, and French. After finishing the entire Latin curriculum, our student investigates his options at local schools and community colleges, finally finding a linguistics class and an advanced Latin class. In addition to his regular course work, this student drives himself to these classes five days a week. He's so good at what he studies and so interested in foreign languages that he takes language classes on the side for three of the four years of high school, plus two summer immersion programs, both in intensive Japanese. By the end of high school, he scores 5 on both the Latin literature advanced placement tests (out of a possible 5), is quite good at Japanese, and garners incredible recommendations from his community college professors, who say he's one of the most natural linguists they have ever seen.

This is initiative. The student could have simply thrown up his hands in frustration that his high school didn't offer language courses that satisfied him, but instead, he went out and did something about it. Not only that, he showed such a passion for the subject that he carved a real niche for himself in the admissions process. Even if his grades aren't perfect, this student is more likely to be accepted to a competitive college than another student with stronger grades who didn't show this level of initiative. In general, if you can be summed up in one key phrase, you will be remembered in the admissions process and you will stand out. Our language student would be known to any admissions officer as the "linguistic genius from Florida"—a great tag line that would practically guarantee him admission as long as he had a strong overall academic record to match.

Since roughly the late 1990s, the focus has shifted away from well-rounded students to the idea of a well-rounded freshman class. The truth was that the Eagle Scout tri-captains were a dime a dozen—colleges needed more to make their class truly shine. Besides filling their sports teams, colleges need to fill their musical groups, dance groups, political groups, debate teams, fraternities, sororities, and dozens of other organizations. I worked with one student who got into Cornell even though she was only a solid student with one major activity. But that activity (Olympic-level gymnastics) was quite unusual. It took up so much of her high school time that she had to enroll in a special program in a different city from where she lived just to finish her high school courses and train at the same time. She held few leadership positions and did no other major school activities. It didn't matter because she was world-class in a specific area. Cornell was happy to have her in its freshman class.

The prevailing philosophy of college admissions for the past twenty years has been that well-rounded students are the most attractive: the student athlete, captain of a few sports, who is also class president and plays piano. Unfortunately, that student would be considered only average in the most selective college applicant pool today.

Though this example is a bit extreme, I've had clients who are exceptional in one particular area—maybe directing plays, music, Web development, or sports—who have chosen to focus on a few key areas of interest in their activity charts. Keep in mind that it's better to emphasize a few areas of major importance rather than a long list of insignificant activities. This will be the overriding philosophy of completing an activity chart.

 ## IS FORMAT IMPORTANT?

In a word, yes. Colleges do not want résumés. In fact they consider it somewhat presumptuous on students' part to think they are important enough to have a résumé in the first place. Résumés are for the *workplace*, not for the college admissions process, so don't submit one.

The correct format to summarize all your extracurricular activities—including leadership, work experience, summer programs, sports, and music—is an activity chart that mimics the one provided on the Common Application form. Before we delve into the details of the chart, it's worth a small detour into what the Common Application is and is not.

The Common Application

Wouldn't it be nice, reasoned students and parents, if all colleges used the same admissions forms so that students didn't have to keep filling out the same information for every single college they applied to? Sure it would, but when the idea was first proposed about twenty-five years ago, only a handful of schools adopted the form. Even today, only about three hundred colleges out of several thousand accept the Common Application. Here's what the Common Application people have to say about their forms:

> Once completed online or in print, copies of the Application for Undergraduate Admission can be sent to any number of participating colleges. . . . Millions of Common Applications are printed and accepted by our members each year. . . . Our college and university members have worked together over the past thirty years to develop the application. All members fully support its use, and all give equal consideration to the Common Application and the college's own form. Many of our members use the Common Application as their only undergraduate admission application.

To make matters even more complicated, many schools have what they call supplementary forms to the Common Application, so students find themselves filling out the Common Application plus completing additional essays and questions for the supplement. In fact, more than 183 of the 296 colleges that currently accept the Common Application— more than 60 percent of participating schools—*require* one or more supplemental essays. Finally, some schools have both their own forms *and* the Common Application. There is very little uniformity in the admissions world. In my opinion, in its present incarnation, the Common Application is a good idea poorly executed. Between supplemental essays (and what's the difference between using these forms and requiring your own distinct application?) and the fact that most colleges don't accept it, I don't see how the Common Application has really streamlined the admissions process for the student.

Colleges will tell you that they treat the Common Application exactly as they do their own application. Nonetheless, I would still encourage you to use the college's own forms if the college honors both, at least for your top choices. I say this because I saw firsthand the downside of the Common Application during my admissions years.

Submitting a Common Application to a school offering both types of forms sends a psychological message that the student is not as interested in attending that school. After all, if Princeton is your first-choice school, why not take the extra time to obtain the Princeton application? Again, colleges are not allowed to discriminate and may not do so on a conscious level, but why take a chance? Until a college does away completely with its own forms (as Harvard and Johns Hopkins have done), just get the forms from the school's Web site. Nowadays most schools have their application available in Adobe Acrobat PDF files (free software you can download from www.adobe.com) on their Web sites, so it's easier than ever to print out the forms.

As I said, some colleges (such as Harvard) use only the Common Application, so you can't go wrong. There's no rhyme or reason as to which schools accept the Common Application and which ones don't. The quickest and easiest way to find out what colleges on your list do take the Common Application is to point your browser to www.commonapp.org. The helpful chart on the Web site provides a summary of due dates and supplementary materials that you can download directly. Here is a list for 2006–7 of Common Application exclusive users. Note that only 24 percent of Common Application schools fall into the exclusive-user category!

COMMON APPLICATION 2006–7 EXCLUSIVE USERS

1. Amherst College
2. Babson College
3. Barnard College
4. Bates College
5. Bennington College
6. Boston College
7. Boston University
8. Bowdoin College
9. Bryn Mawr College
10. Bucknell College
11. Caltech
12. Carleton College
13. Carnegie Mellon University
14. Carnegie Mellon University in Qatar
15. Champlain College
16. Claremont McKenna College
17. Clarkson University
18. Colby College
19. Colgate University
20. Concordia College (New York)
21. Connecticut College
22. Cornell University
23. Dartmouth College
24. Denison University
25. Dickinson College
26. Duke University
27. Franklin and Marshall College
28. Furman University
29. Gettysburg College
30. Grinnell College
31. Hamilton College
32. Harvard College
33. Haverford College
34. Hobart and William Smith Colleges
35. Juniata College
36. Kenyon College
37. Lafayette College
38. Lehigh University
39. Linfield University
40. Marlboro College
41. Miami University (Ohio)
42. Middlebury College
43. Millsaps College
44. Mount Holyoke College
45. Muhlenberg College
46. Notre Dame de Namur University
47. Oberlin College
48. Pitzer College
49. Pomona College
50. Providence College
51. Reed College
52. Richmond, University of
53. Roger Williams University
54. St. Lawrence University
55. St. Olaf College
56. Santa Clara University
57. Sarah Lawrence College
58. Seattle University
59. Skidmore College
60. Smith College
61. Susquehanna University
62. Swarthmore College
63. Trinity University (San Antonio)
64. Union College (New York)
65. Villanova University
66. Washington University in Saint Louis
67. Wellesley College
68. Wesleyan University
69. Whitman College
70. Willamette University
71. Williams College
72. Wooster, College of
73. Yale University

It's fair to use the Common Application format guidelines for your activity list even if you are not using the Common Application. The Common Application gives the following directions:

Extracurricular, Personal, and Volunteer Activities (Including Summer)

Please list your **principal** extracurricular, community, and family activities and hobbies **in the order of their interest to you.** Include specific events and/or major accomplishments such as musical instrument played, varsity letters earned, etc. Check (✓) in the right column (PS) those activities you hope to pursue in college. **To allow us to focus on the highlights of your activities, please complete this section even if you plan to attach a résumé.**

First of all, as I have emphasized, *never* attach a résumé. Second of all, you will have to summarize your activity list on this form, but when we are done you will see why the activity list I suggest is infinitely more helpful than the basic chart. After the above directions comes a very basic grid with the table headings shown on page 13.

The first thing you may notice is that there is not much room to elaborate. For some things, no elaboration is needed. If you are captain of the varsity soccer team, most colleges will understand the category of varsity soccer, and then the

Activity	Grade level or post-secondary					Approx. time spent		Positions held, honors won, or letters earned
	9	10	11	12	PS	Hours per week	Weeks per year	

position of captain. However, some activities are not familiar to everyone. What if you worked with an unknown charity group, started a poetry club in your school, or trained Seeing Eye dogs? A chart this minimal will simply not do justice to these activities or explain your depth of involvement.

That is why the first thing I have my clients do is work on a more detailed (but not overly so) activity list that fleshes out some of their activities. In the interest of space, you don't need to have separate columns for grades 9,10,11, 12, and PS—one column will do in which you simply write in 9–10, 9–11, or whatever grades you participated. Though you can use a variety of fancy programs, Microsoft Word is very easy to format. If you use the "Table" function on the main menu and select "Insert Table," you will be able to punch in the number of rows and columns and voilà, you have a chart. Then all you have to do is line up your cursor on the vertical lines until the symbol changes and drag the vertical lines left and right to leave yourself more space in the last column.

For every entry, your opening descriptive sentences should give a brief statement of what the activity is. (Don't bother if it's something everyone knows, such as soccer or football.) Then describe your specific leadership role in the form of, "As president, I was responsible for x, y, and z." No need to ramble here—be precise and to the point. Include any major awards or accolades right in your description.

Sample Activity Sheets

Let's take a look at an actual sample of one of my very first clients, who was admitted to Columbia. As you can see from his activity list, he is an extraordinary guy. On a scale of 1 to 9 with 9 being the highest, this ranks an academic 9. Don't worry if yours is not this detailed—hardly anyone accomplishes this in their lifetime, much less in high school. Think of this chart as the ultimate version of what is typically more modest and less spectacular.

Sample Activity Sheet
EMPLOYMENT

Company	Years Active (hours per week)	Position	Description
The Entertainment Group	11-12 (never-ending!)	Assistant Director Pyrotechnic Operator	My major time commitment takes place outside of school. Driven by my passion for all facets of the theater, I branched out to new areas, specifically directing and theatrical production. In my role as assistant director in a professional production, I am required to manage the actors and technicians, as well as to maintain a prompt book, which holds all cues for the final performance. Additionally, after the director had staged a specific scene, it was my responsibility to clean the scene, ensuring a professional product. Lastly, during the performance, I detonated many large explosive devices, which produced a mystical flarelike effect.
The Entertainment Group	10-12 (45 during summer)	Counselor	Providing an opportunity to impart my knowledge of the theater to others, I was employed by the children's theater division of the Entertainment Group. Please note that this division is distinct from the above. Within this division, experienced actors lead a summer camp that specializes in theatrical technique. As a counselor, I served as an adviser between the instructors and the sixty-six students whom I managed for a period of eight weeks.

SCHOOL-SPONSORED NONACADEMIC ACTIVITIES

Activity	Years Active (hours per week)	Position	Description
The International Thespian Society	10-12 (20-25)	Senior: President Junior: Honor Bar Recipient Sophomore: Charter Member	The International Thespian Society is an internationally renowned organization of actors and technicians that holds yearly competitions to judge individual and ensemble performance. As president of the society, my responsibilities include organizing educational workshops, supervising fund-raising activities, representing our troupe in all district and state affairs, conducting weekly meetings, and encouraging members to participate actively in the theater.
The National Honor Society	11-12 (3-8)	Senior: President Junior: Vice President Charter Member	As a charter member and president of our National Honor Society, I am accountable for creating and strengthening our chapter of the national organization. To ensure the existence of a strong, coherent society, I have initiated traditions and set precedents, which will be utilized by future members of the organization. For example, I, with the assistance of the board, have written our society's constitution and bylaws. I established fund-raising techniques (i.e., the penny war) that have become annual NHS fund-raisers.

Activity	Years Active	Position	Description
	(hours per week)		
Pre-Medical Club	11-12 (1-2)	Senior: Member Junior: Charter Member	The Pre-Med Club, which holds bimonthly meetings, is an organization of students interested in the medical profession. Some members intend to actively pursue a career in medicine, while others, including myself, are simply interested in the medical profession. During meetings, members visit a physician at a local hospital or research facility, follow the doctor's afternoon routine, and partake in a lecture session.
Key Club International	11-12 (2-3)	Senior: Co-Supervisor of Blood Drive Junior: Charter Member	Key Club International, sponsored by the local Kiwanis chapter, is a community outreach program that encourages student participation in community service. Personally, I have been responsible for organizing the annual blood drive at a local bank and for bolstering student involvement in programs like fund-raising walks for cancer research.

Activity	Years Active	Position	Description
	(hours per week)		
AIDS Awareness Week	11-12 (15 hours for a duration of 2 weeks)	Senior/ Junior: Creator, Founder, and Chair	I have seen the ravages of AIDS firsthand. Hoping to explain the dangers of AIDS and to debunk false information, I initiated a collaborative effort with a local health clinic, run by the Red Cross, to bring an annual AIDS Awareness Week to my school. With a fund-raiser, a theatrical performance, and an information session with an AIDS counselor, the week was a huge success. We raised money for a local AIDS shelter, while arming students with essential facts.
Academic Council	12 (2)	Senior: Chair	To ameliorate relations between drama students and faculty, an academic council was established to discuss issues ranging from attendance policy to work extensions. As chair, I am ultimately responsible for expressing the students' beliefs and debating in their favor to the administration.

Activity	Years Active	Position	Description
	(hours per week)		
General School Service	10–12 (varies)	N/A	Due to the nature of our school, specific clubs have not been assigned specific school duties, such as prospective student orientation and tours. Therefore, individuals are chosen by administrators to accomplish these tasks. Fulfilling my *required* community hours (30 total/10 in-school), I frequently volunteer to assist in school programs, such as traffic direction, student orientation, et cetera.
Model United Nations	11 (varies)	Junior: Charter Member	Representing my school in conferences such as the Connecticut United Nations Simulation, I exercised my interest in international politics, while promoting the school. My responsibilities as a member of the Model UN include assisting others with preparation, partaking in discussion related to international affairs, and gaining positive support from the school community.

Activity	Years Active (hours per week)	Position	Description
Honor Code Committee	11 (varies)	Junior: Member	Based on a college honor code, the Honor Code of our school community is central to our school's operation. The code was created by students and is enforced by students. To ensure the proper use of this document, a committee was established to analyze the effectiveness of the document and its current interpretation in order to prevent abuses. As a member, I suggested a major alteration in the application of the document's principles, which led to a revision of Honor Code procedure.
Honor Code Court	11 (8 hours when in session)	Junior: Jury Panelist	When acts punishable under the Honor Code are committed, the accused student is entitled to a hearing and judgment by peers. As a leader in my school community with high ethical credibility, I was chosen to be a member of the adjudicating panel.

Activity	Years Active (hours per week)	Position	Description
El Club de Español	11-12 (1-2)	Junior: Charter Member	The Spanish Club was created to expose its members to the various facets of Spanish culture. As a charter member, I was responsible for setting precedents with regard to club activities and encouraging the participation and involvement of the school community.
Student Privileges Committee	10-11 (1-3)	Junior: Member Sophomore: Member	As our school began its initial expansion, a committee was created to allow an outlet for student desires. We voiced concerns and suggested areas of improvement, which were in turn improved upon by the administration.
Drama Club	9 (10-20)	Freshman: President-Elect, Member	I was heavily involved in the Drama Club at a neighboring high school. Starring as Marcellus Washburn in *The Music Man* and Scrooge in *A Christmas Carol*, I was one of the few freshmen to participate. Despite my lack of seniority, I was elected president later that year. However, due to my transfer to my current high school, I was not able to fulfill my presidency.

COMMUNITY INVOLVEMENT

Activity	Years Active (hours per week)	Description
The Entertainment Group	7-12 (15-20 during active season)	Fulfilling my passion for the theater, I have spent and continue to spend large amounts of time and effort at this local theater company. Beginning with this company at the age of twelve, I have progressed through the ranks, and currently hold a position on the staff. Starring in productions ranging from *Anything Goes* to *A Chorus Line*, I have experienced the rigors of community, children's, and professional theater. Additionally, with this company I have been exposed to various aspects of the theater. Through this exposure and experimentation, I have discovered my principal interest in theatrical direction and production.
AIDS Charity Collection	12 (varies)	In conjunction with Connecticut's Thespian District 9, I initiated an AIDS charity collection during district competition. During the two-day competition, a fund-raising raffle will be held for various theatrical prizes. All of the collected monies will be donated to Equity Fights AIDS, a national division of the actors union devoted to providing care for actors and technicians who have developed AIDS.

Activity	Years Active (hours per week)	Description
Hospital Visitation	11-12 (varies)	In a joint effort with the Eucharistic ministry at my church, I visit the local hospital on a triweekly basis. During these sessions, I generally attempt to provide conversation and happiness to the otherwise lonely patients.

EXTRACURRICULAR ACADEMIC ACTIVITIES

Class	Years Active (hours per week)	Description
Dale Carnegie Training	11 (6 for the class's duration)	Taking advantage of the opportunity to solidify my basic understanding of relationships and management, I attended a Dale Carnegie Training seminar. During the eight-week class, I further explored the issues of guidance, control, and positive relationships. With the skills obtained from this class, I learned how to influence others, convey ideas precisely, and manage a wide variety of personal relationships.

PLEASE NOTE: The actual chart on 8 ½ × 11 inch paper should be no more than three pages.

Needless to say, Eric was a top student—I knew him more personally than some of my regular clients because he was also my student in English class. On a scale of 1 to 9 of extracurricular involvement, he'd certainly be an 8 or 9. Let's look at what he communicates to an admissions office. First of all, because many of his most important activities in theater take place outside of school, he makes a separate category and lists them first. In general, students should list their most important categories first, and then within each category list the activities from most meaningful to least meaningful. The Entertainment Group is not self-explanatory, which is why Eric elaborates on what the group itself is and what his responsibilities were as part of it. An admissions officer would give Eric points for his unusual focus on directing rather than acting. Note how he even adds some light touches such as his pyrotechnic prowess—no need to put admissions officers to sleep.

The next positive an admissions office would notice in Eric's long list of in-school nonacademic activities is that he is more often than not a leader and charter member of societies and clubs. Even in more conventional clubs, such as the National Honor Society, Eric's contributions are far from conventional—he wrote all the bylaws for the society. His list presents him as a pathfinder, establishing many new traditions at a relatively new school. Having seen him in action, I can attest to the fact that he seemed to be everywhere at once. In addition, there is some relation and overlap, particularly in theater, that tie together his in-school and out-of-school activities.

In the community service category, an admissions officer would once again spot Eric's initiative—he came up with the idea of raising funds for AIDS research and carried out a successful fund-raiser. I think it's commendable that Eric specifically mentions which activities were part of his required community service as opposed to others he did on his own (showing more initiative). Students often ask me, "Aren't colleges impressed by community service?" Sure, they are impressed, but not any more than they are by other activities. In fact, now that many high schools do require community service, the value is somewhat lowered for admissions purposes because it is obvious that students had to participate. This is not to say that students should drop their community service activities. Remember this key piece of advice: You should never drop an activity you like or add an activity you don't like just to please an admissions committee. If you gain personal satisfaction out of doing community service (or any other activity), involve yourself in it. If you find that you really do not gain anything from one of your activities, drop it so you can spend more time on things that are important to you. Passion cannot be faked, at least not very well. It will be obvious to an admissions officer whether you love what you do or just do it because you have to.

Take a moment to reread Eric's activity list—his excitement, passion, and talent are emphasized throughout. He does an excellent job of balancing his descriptions between what the club involves on a general level and what his contributions were specifically. His directing talents have gone beyond the local level to a state/international level with the thespian group and he has devoted substantial time to the activities he loves. Note that he lists only the clubs in which he had major leadership roles. For the most part, students should leave out clubs they only joined for a short period of time or clubs where they were basically just members who met for only an hour a week.

On the next pages is another one of my favorite activity lists. Notice how it communicates passion and initiative.

MUSIC

Activity	Grades Active (hours per week)	Position	Description
Jazz Band	10–12 (2)	Sophomore–Senior: 1st Chair Drum Set	Our jazz band is a very high-level performing group that plays everything from jazz standards (*New Orleans Suite*) to funk ("Pick Up the Pieces") to original compositions ("Test Pilots" by local composer John Lissauer). We were selected to perform at both the West Point Jazz Festival and the All-County Jazz Concert. As principal drum set player for the last three years, I have helped the band achieve a higher level of musicianship.
Marching Band	9–12 (12 during season)	Senior: Drum Line Captain Junior: Asst. Drum Line Captain Sophomore: Asst. Drum Line Captain Freshman: Drum Line	Although we are a small band (thirty members), we make a big sound. We were crowned EMBA Division I Champions this year and won several local competitions. As drum captain, I have helped the drum line become the featured band section. Although I've played every percussion instrument over the years, my main focus remains the tenor drums (quads and quints).

Activity	Years Active (hours per week)	Position	Description
Pit Orchestra	9–12 (12 during weeks of musical)	Senior/ Junior: Principal Percussionist Sophomore: Principal Percussionist Freshman: Auxiliary Percussion	Although playing in a pit orchestra can be very stressful, it can also be fun. We play in the "pit" for the school's full production spring musicals. Freshman year, I was the auxiliary percussionist for *Guys and Dolls*. My sophomore and junior years, I was the principal percussionist (playing drum set, mallets, and auxiliary) for *Anything Goes* and *Pirates of Penzance*.
Music Composition	9–12	n/a	I have always had a passion for composing music. Throughout high school, I have composed several pieces in a variety of genres (string quartet, choir, band, electronica) for my music theory classes and for my own enjoyment. This year, I am taking an independent study in music composition so that I can have time every school day to devote to the intense process of original composition.

Activity	Years Active (hours per week)	Position	Description
Area All-State Band/ Orchestra	10-12 (5 during weeks before performance)	Senior/ Junior: Orchestra: Principal Timpanist Alternate to All-State Band Sophomore: Band: Principal Timpanist	To be selected into these elite groups, I went through a rigorous audition process. I had the opportunity to practice and perform with the best musicians in my county. Playing timpani, I was a featured musician in many of the pieces, including *West Side Story* and *Songs of Earth, Fire, Water, and Sky* (timpani and djembe, an African drum)
Concert Band	9-12 (5)	Freshman- Senior: Principal Percussionist	During my time in high school, the band has played some pretty amazing pieces. As principal percussionist for four years, it was (and is still) my duty to ensure that all the parts were covered and that the other musicians knew their parts. I also assist the band director by teaching my fellow percussionists some of the more challenging parts (after all, there's nothing worse than an extra cymbal shot after the conductor has cut the band).

Activity	Years Active (hours per week)	Position	Description
Percussion Ensemble	11-12 (3)	Senior/ Junior: Principal Marimba	The percussion ensemble only started up in 2002, but it quickly became a strong performing group. Although we didn't compete officially this year, we hope to in 2003. In addition to playing the principal marimba parts, I taught another musician how to transfer his piano abilities to the marimba.
Orchestra	10-12 (2)	Sophomore/ Junior: Violist	The orchestra program at my school is small but growing rapidly. In response to a violist shortage, I decided to join the group and tackle a new instrument. Although I found viola to be more difficult than percussion, I enjoyed the opportunity to play with an orchestra. It not only helped bolster my musicianship, it also helped me to become a better composer.

SCHOOL CLUBS AND ORGANIZATIONS

Activity	Years Active (hours per week)	Position	Description
Student Government	9-12 (varies)	Senior: Senior Class Secretary Junior: Community Service Coordinator on Executive Board Sophomore: PTSA Rep. to Executive Board Freshman: Freshman Class Rep. to Executive Board	Holding several positions on the class board and the executive board has allowed me to take on leadership roles in many areas. As community service coordinator, I helped to organize a walk-a-thon team to support breast and ovarian cancer research. As senior class secretary, I hope to create greater class unity.

Activity	Years Active	Position	Description
	(hours per week)		
National Honor Society	10–12 (varies)	Senior: President Junior: Junior Representative Sophomore: Candidate, Member	Although National Honor Societies sometimes can be titular in nature, our school's group is very active. As junior representative, I helped to organize and run a tutoring service in which NHS members tutored children in lower grades and high school students in lower-level classes. This year as president, my goal is to train the other members in leadership skills so they can have a greater effect both in school and in the community.
Tusker Times (School Newspaper)	10–12 (varies)	Senior/ Junior: Features Co-Editor Sophomore: Staff Writer	As both an editor and a writer for the paper, I was able to immerse myself in the world of journalism. In my capacity as staff writer, I have written several humorous pieces that poke fun at some of the absurdities of our school (i.e., a big golden sign over the lunch room that boasts "CAFETERIA"). One of my articles on clichés was mentioned in the *Journal News*, a local newspaper.

Activity	Years Active (hours per week)	Position	Description
French National Honor Society	10–12	Sophomore/ Senior: Member	I was inducted into this organization after my third year of French. Although the group does not hold formal meetings, it is responsible for helping tutor lower-level French students.
French Club	9–12	Freshman– Senior: Member	As a member of this club for four years, I have helped to organize both Mardi Gras festivals and yearly cultural trips.

SPECIAL PROGRAMS

Program	Years Active (hours per week)	Description
Berklee College of Music 5-Week Summer Performance Program	Summer 2002	This past summer, I decided to bolster my musical abilities by attending the five-week summer performance program at the Berklee College of Music in Boston. The program was run much like a regular semester at the college in that I took classes (theory, musicianship, etc.) and performed in ensembles (salsa and jazz). Throughout the course of the five weeks, I honed my ear training and jazz theory skills. I also made vast improvements on drum set, congas, and djembe. I'm excited to see how I can use my new skills to improve the overall quality of the many high school ensembles I perform with.

Program	Years Active (hours per week)	Description
Presidential Classroom	11 (1-week program)	Presidential Classroom brings together students from all across the country to meet with each other and with several high-ranking guest speakers in Washington, D.C. The highlight of the week was helping my friend win the mock presidential election by working with him on writing and perfecting his speech.
Hugh O'Brian Youth Leadership Program	10 (3-day program)	HOBY is a leadership program that brings together sophomores from neighboring counties in order to educate them in community service and leadership. At HOBY I was able to listen to guest speakers who showed me not only the importance of giving back to one's community but also the particulars of how to lead and organize service projects. I used my experience to help organize a school supplies drive that summer.
Junior Peer Communication Workshop	11 (2-day program)	During this seminar, the entire junior class was taken into the woods for two days. Through topic discussions, skits, and trust activities, we interacted with members of our class with whom we usually never even spoke. The ultimate objective of the workshop was to bring the class together into a more cohesive unit. The last activity, a very emotional one during which everyone sat in a circle and shared something meaningful, showed me just how far our class had come in terms of class unity in such a short span of time.

Program	Years Active	Description
	(hours per week)	
JOURNEY Program	11 (1-day program)	JOURNEY brought together juniors from my school with rising ninth graders. Working with students from another high school, we answered the students' questions and discussed with them some of the difficult issues and situations that they may confront in high school.
Union Council for Human Rights Conference	10 (1-day program)	This one-day seminar focused on human rights violations in the United States and abroad.

EMPLOYMENT

Company	Years Active (hours per week)	Position	Description
Northern Music School Inc.	11-12 (6-7)	Percussion Teacher	This job is perfect for me because it combines my love of music with my love of teaching. Teaching upward of ten lessons a week to twelve students, I am really able to work with my students and instill in them a love of drumming. I teach them not only how to play the drums but also how to develop good musicianship through practicing and developing their technique.
Summer Trails Day Camp	(40 hrs. during summer '01)	Counselor	Third-grade boys can be very difficult to keep up with, but on this job getting tired was not an option. I thoroughly enjoyed being a camp counselor at a day camp. The highlight of my summer was an impromptu drum lesson that I gave my group on a makeshift set of tables, chairs, and plastic percussion instruments. The performance was well received by a group of counselors and campers who were on their way to lunch.
Hebrew and Math Tutor	9-12	Tutor	Once a week, I tutor a fourth-grade boy in Hebrew and math. Since I have started tutoring him, his Hebrew reading ability (and, subsequently, mine as well) has significantly improved. He has also become better at facing and handling challenging math problems.

This chart shows how John highlighted his very high level of musicianship—clearly he would add to any college's music department. Many of his activities centered around music, but that's *great*, because it shows his excellence in that one particular area. He shows a great deal of initiative in *all* his activities—look at how he actually picked up and learned how to play the viola, an instrument far removed from the drums in technique. Finally, he was a leader in his school, used his summers to build on his interests, and showed hands-on work experience. John was admitted early decision to Dartmouth College.

Should You Lie or Exaggerate?

In a word, no. The issue brings up an important point about honesty and integrity. Admissions officers are not stupid. If Eric or John had described all his activities, but then not one school person (out of two teacher recommendations, a counselor recommendation, or even extra ones from theater groups) even mentioned that he was a campus leader, admissions officers might suspect Eric or John of lying. Of course, as I know from personal experience, Eric was *the* campus leader—every letter of reference (including one I wrote for him) could not fail to comment that he was not only the school's top student, he was the school's top leader as well. In addition, he happened to be a super-nice boy with a real intellectual bent. Students should keep in mind that their schools provide some of the most important information about them through recommendation letters. If a student says he was elected class president, that fact should be substantiated through people from the school. Not every fact will be verified, but general leadership trends certainly will. It is clear not just from their own activity lists but also from what teachers and counselors say about them that Eric and John are high-impact presences on campus. Represent your activities honestly. Admissions officers have BS detectors for résumé stuffers, exaggerators, and aggrandizers. The key is to actually *be* a leader, an initiator, and a role model, not to misrepresent yourself as such. Substance will always win out over fluff.

The Benefit of Work Experience

Although admissions personnel don't like to admit it, they do harbor a prejudice against privileged students who (as they perceive it) have had many things simply handed to them on a silver platter. Their thinking goes something like, "How can this student show initiative when every time he's ever wanted something, someone simply gave it to him?" It doesn't help that the majority of admissions officers do not come from upper-crust backgrounds—there are more working-class admissions officers than scions of the investment banker crowd. Whether consciously or unconsciously, admissions officers have higher expectations for students who have not had to struggle to get where they are now, a pretty commonsense approach. This prejudice works against students from plush addresses (Fifth Avenue in New York City, Greenwich in Connecticut) or from fancy private schools who may have the additional misfortune of having a "III" affixed to their names.

Whether you like it or not, if you have had every possible advantage, you will have to do all that you can to fight this prejudice. One of the best ways to do this is to hold a steady job, the less exalted the better. Let me recount an incident I remember from the Ivy League admissions conference. One director used to talk about his summers spent lugging packages for a delivery service. He told the story often enough to make it clear that he valued work because he himself had to work to help pay for school and life expenses. Many in other Ivy offices had similar experiences. Often in committee when we sat around a table with the onerous task of accepting only one out of six or seven students, there would be a moment of silence and then someone would ask, "Well, has he ever *worked?*"

When I say work, I really don't mean a fancy job in your mother's or father's law firm, because that won't help you much in the bias department—they will just assume that Mommy or Daddy pulled some strings and got you a job. The best kind of jobs are those that tie in to your field of interest: a hockey player who works in a sporting goods store, a musician who works in Sam Ash. As with anything else in the activity list, you don't want to start in your junior year because then it will look like you got a job *only* for admissions purposes. I'd recommend finding a job as early as possible (eighth, ninth grade) and working part time during the year with more hours in summers. You want to establish continuity rather than a one-time burst of activity. Avoid glamorous jobs that are clearly the result of a parent pulling strings for you because that only reinforces the silver spoon image. This is the time to pound the proverbial pavement.

If you aren't crazy about working for someone else, start your own business in a field that relates to your academic interests. Let's look at some real examples by excerpting some job descriptions from students I've worked with. The following is an excellent example of a practical job that would enhance the student's status in the eyes of an admissions officer:

> I have been helping my parents on our farm in Cambridge County all my life, with tasks ranging from animal care to manual labor around the property. Most of my work in the summer, when I am home the most, is centered on cutting and baling hay. Our farm produces small square bales and the larger round bales, which require the use of heavy machinery (tractors, balers, and mechanical rakes) along with long hours of patience and hard work. When I'm not involved in the hay harvest, my mother (she runs the farm) has me busy with any type of work she can find—this summer it's been mostly digging holes for bamboo plants, helping with the construction of our barn, and assisting a

carpenter in rebuilding some of the older structures around the farm. This job is my main source of income year-round, and remains my main source of employment since my labor is needed too much for me to seek a summer job elsewhere.

Clearly we are not dealing with a privileged student; he's spent time both during the year and almost every summer doing manual labor for his family. Even though this student did attend a well-known boarding school, he emphasized his ties to the land, which take up a significant amount of time. By adding that he does this job every summer, he also explains why he has not spent his summers on fancy trips or big-name summer academic programs. Even in these brief sentences, the student's very likable personality also shines through.

Other students choose to emphasize a job born out of a particular talent or field of expertise. This next student describes how his interest in graphic design took him to a professional job and his own business neither of which resulted from parental intervention.

I convinced X, a twenty-five-employee Web development firm in "Manyard," New York, to hire me despite my age (I was the youngest by five years they had ever hired). I work with the other Web design professionals, client managers, and systems administrators to develop Web sites and graphical user interfaces for a variety of major companies. During my two years at the company, I designed over fifteen sites, including x, y, and z. In my position as Web designer, I am in charge of developing the visual look of sites (via graphics software such as Adobe Photoshop), working with programmers on functionality, and using elements such as Macromedia Flash animation, HTML, and JavaScript to put the site together. After my experience at X, I noticed a need for high-impact, professional, and affordable Web site design in the Manyard area. Many local businesses expressed an interest in establishing a Web presence and offered to hire me. As a result, I started my own company, KidWeb LLC. We work with a wide client base, ranging from a one-partner law firm to a thirty-person lawn maintenance company. I run KidWeb during both the academic year and the summer and plan to expand the business during college. Due to high demand, I recruited and hired two of my friends as client managers. Now we are a powerful three-man operation with a rapidly increasing profit margin.

This student would impress the admissions committee on several fronts. First off, his passion for graphic design shows through. Second, he's reached a very high level of competence—so much so that he was the only student hired in a small professional company. Finally, he shows a high level of initiative by taking this first experience and expanding it into his own business, a task that sometimes takes more than thirty hours a week, all during the school year. This student is a mover and a shaker, a good prospect as a high impact player at any college. The graphic design thread ran all through his application from his academic course work in math and computer science, his extracurricular activities, and his work activities. Because his academic record was equally impressive, he is now at an Ivy League school.

In the next example, we see yet another student who stands out because of an interest in computers and technology that was present all through the application, not just in the activity sheet description.

I have always been attracted to computers and new technology. I have taken classes in computer programming and computer science (including the time I spent at Duke University's Talent Identification Program). These classes compelled me to learn more about the inner workings of computers. I apprenticed with a computer technician in order to learn how to troubleshoot, upgrade, and fix computers. Then I completed a 250-hour class for A+ certification, which certified me as a qualified computer technician. Using parts that I ordered from computer warehouses, I assembled the computer I currently use from scratch. When I go into a bookstore, I often find myself spending money on computer books to learn a new language or a new skill. In my free time I have taught myself Flash, Adobe Photoshop, basic C++, and 3D Studio Max.

There are several elements here worthy of note: The student's achievements and initiative are substantial. Rather than just taking the usual short computer course, this student took an adult-oriented class with 250 hours of instruction. That's a serious time commitment. Using the knowledge from his class, he assembled his own computer, which shows even more initiative and expertise—he ordered all the parts, put it together, and then used it for all his own work. In addition, we see an obvious love of learning—in his spare time he teaches himself new computer languages and complex programming skills, builds machines, and seeks out additional challenges like the nationally respected Duke Talent Identification Program. Many students make the mistake of thinking that one single activity such as Duke's academic program will add to their application, but they are not quite correct. What's really impressive is the weaving together of several related activities with a common thread, as we see here. The student didn't simply sign himself up for a Duke summer program; rather, he actively sought out challenging experiences in computers and technologies in school, in his spare time, and in other academic settings.

Let's look at one final example of work experience:

All last summer I worked the counter at a store called Packages Plus. My main responsibilities included ringing up purchases, using a computer to determine the weight and shipping price for the package, entering the appropriate shipping information, and repackaging items that were improperly packaged. When business was slow I took it upon myself to create new and innovative advertisement flyers for the store that increased traffic noticeably.

Clearly this student took a grunt job that consisted of mostly menial work, but it did tie in to some of his other interests like computer programming, graphic design, and his general show of initiative. Even in this brief description we get the sense that when this student sees something that needs fixing, he immediately looks for a solution.

What About Strange and Unusual Hobbies?

The more strange and unusual, the better. I've had students who have been avid motorcycle riders, kite flyers, glassblowers, English-horn players, stamp collectors, poetry slam organizers—the more unusual, the more you will be remembered in the admissions process. In fact, it may surprise you to know that admissions directors are constantly searching for students with oddball activities or interests because at the end of the admissions season, all directors have to prepare a summary report on the prospective class. In addition to including statistical information (how many valedictorians, salutatorians, members of the top 10 percent of their class), directors like to throw in some descriptions of the more interesting accepted students. It would not be uncommon to hear, "Not only is this class the best academic class we have had in the last twenty years, but our class includes a fire thrower, a champion mogul jumper, a nationally recognized poet, the nation's top debater, an Internet CEO of a start-up e-mail business, and a published author." Look at any admissions summary (usually printed in the college's daily newspaper) and you will find equivalent descriptions at most every school. Your job then is to aim for one of these coveted listings if you happen to have a high level of competence or just an unusual talent or hobby.

Some of the impact of these activities has to do with what I call the bond-of-commonality theory of life: We tend to notice others with interests similar to ours. For example, an admissions officer who is an avid backyard astronomer will be immediately impressed by a student who writes about his telescope, astronomy interest, and passion for the stars. Former high school athletes will be impressed by athletic prowess; classicists will give the nod to students with high interest in Latin and Greek. No matter how objective we try to be, it is human nature to search for a common bond.

In addition to the bond of commonality (and the off chance that someone in the admissions office grew up racing model race cars like you), hobbies can emphasize intellectual qualities that may not be apparent in the academic part of the application (or it can emphasize a quality that *is* apparent in the academic section). Some hobbies (computers, puzzles, building engines, scientific research) have an academic focus that show a student's pursuit of upper-level brain activities outside the confines of the classroom. Then there are those hobbies that are simply fun, with little or no academic component—that's fine, too. This is an example of the latter:

> I have been hunting and participating in outdoor sports since I was little. Skeet shooting has proved to be a great way to practice and improve my shooting year-round. A nearby resort has a skeet range where I shoot skeet, sporting clays, and variations of other challenging shooting events. Skeet shooting requires patience, practice, and above all else a high consciousness of safety. After years of shooting, I'm close to my objective of shooting a perfect round of twenty-five (breaking all twenty-five "birds").

Although one might argue that shooting does take a certain amount of intellectual energy, in this case it's clear that the student loves the challenge and release of skeet shooting. I've done it myself and there are few things in life as satisfying as breaking that orange disc into smithereens. Let's look at another definitively nonacademic hobby that nonetheless adds something to this student's application:

As a hobby I enjoy working on my Honda Accord coupe as well as my friends' cars. I have performed modifications on everything from a Honda Civic to a BMW. These modifications include things such as installing sound systems, custom headlights, custom taillights, exhaust systems, grilles, oil changes, tire rotations, and wheel changes. Over the years I have taken a few automotive classes pertaining to regular maintenance. All of my experience makes me a good person to have around if your car breaks down.

Playing with cars does take a certain degree of intellect and initiative to learn. What I like about this description is that it's not at all pretentious—in fact, it makes the applicant seem quite down to earth and likable. The student does throw in that he has taken some classes, too, but he's not trying to say that it's an academic hobby. The touch of humor at the end hits just the right note. Humor in light doses is always welcome.

Think long and hard about your passions outside of school. Some examples of hobbies that should definitely be included are mountain climbing, sport fishing, collecting (stamps, coins, or anything else), stargazing, hiking, cooking, baking, or anything else that brings out a different side of you. Listing (with a brief explanation of the depth of your involvement) your hobbies and side pursuits is a good way to round out your activity list as well as to shed some light on what you are really interested in besides school.

Summary

The activity list is one of the most crucial parts of the whole application because it establishes the student's talents, passions, interest level, and impact on his or her local community. The key is depth and breadth, not length. It is far better to have a few passionate interests than scores of low-level "joiner" activities. It should be a forum for briefly explaining any nontraditional or unusual activities, interests, hobbies, work experience, or anything else that takes place outside of the school day. Admissions officers are looking for high-impact students, students who will become very involved in their future college's campus life and who will be able to influence and lead those around them. They are also looking for extraordinary talent. Think of the activity list as your chance to have a twenty-minute conversation directly with an admissions officer to explain everything you do that is important to you. For those activities that are unusual, you'll need to give detailed explanations to make clear what your involvement was. The activity list is crucial for students who have significant activities that take place outside of their immediate school environment. If you don't take the time to mention all your commitments and leadership activities, don't expect this information to be magically communicated to colleges.

To sum up the major steps to producing the activity list:

1. Using the "view" command in a program such as Microsoft Word, choose "header/footer" and add a

header that includes your name, Social Security number, date of birth, and high school name so that it will appear in the upper right-hand corner of each page.

2. List all your major activities, hobbies, sports, clubs, et cetera on a piece of paper so you can place them into two to four general categories (for example, work, school clubs, dance, theater).

3. Make your own categories. While one person may have "Squash," "Music," "Employment," you might have "Singing," "Technical Theater," and "Leadership Programs."

4. Then set up a table, being sure to adjust the columns so that the description column is the widest. (Word processing hint: Under "Page setup" you will need to choose "Landscape" rather than "Portrait" so the page aligns itself horizontally, not vertically. Otherwise it will be impossible to fit the columns in two to four pages.)

5. Use a 10- or 11-point font so that you can fit in the descriptions.

6. Follow the categories outlined in the Common Application so you can use the same activity list for every college you apply to.

7. Within each category, list activities from most important to least important or most recent to least recent.

8. As for descriptions, your first sentence should give a quick summary of what the club or organization does. The next sentence should start right in with what you did: "As president of the astronomy club, I organized events . . ."

9. Use a natural, conversational tone of voice—don't be overly formal.

10. If the hours of time per week vary dramatically, you can break it down: two hours during off-season and fifteen during season. Try to be as specific as possible. Be sure to include any interesting hobbies or outside activities that you are genuinely involved in.

11. Avoid the temptation to lie or exaggerate; leave out clubs or activities that involved little or no commitment.

12. Do not comment on what you liked or didn't like. Concentrate on what you actually *did*. Avoid sentences like "It was meaningful to me."

13. Use active verbs, not passive ones: "I collated envelopes, I rounded up one thousand students, and I led the student-run car wash."

14. Be descriptive—no generalities. "As captain, I raised $3,200 through three bake sales and a walkathon."

15. Be sure to highlight truly noteworthy accomplishments or awards that give an indication that what you accomplished was meaningful. For example, "I

was one of three students out of a thousand selected for this position."

16. Don't spell out obvious activities just to fill up space. If you're captain of the soccer team, you do *not* need to write, "Soccer is a team sport played at our school." Instead, focus on what you did as captain.

17. If your sport's team is very competitive, mention the level of competition right in your description: "Our varsity soccer team finished first in the Northeast regional competition for two years in a row, so it was an honor for me to be the starting goalie for those two years."

18. Use your spell checker and have your parents or friends read it to find any careless errors or any activities you left out.

19. Finally, avoid clichés and boring wording—write like yourself. Admissions officers want to get an idea of your depth of involvement.

2

THE WARM-UP ESSAYS

After working on the activity list, it's time to work on some of the smaller essays that make up the application. Though I use the Common Application as my guide, I will suggest additional smaller essays that are good to have for other applications.

 IN-DEPTH ACTIVITY

The first essay the Common Application lists is worded thus:

Please briefly elaborate on one of your activities (extracurricular, personal activities, or work experience).
Attach your response on a separate sheet (150 words or fewer).

To make it easy on yourself, you should always do these essays on a separate sheet of paper, taking care to put your name, Social Security number, date of birth, and high school name at the top of each page (use the header function). Because papers tend to get misfiled in admissions offices, it is always a good idea to have this informaton on every attached page.

Many of the same rules apply to this essay as to the activity list: Admissions officers are still looking for passion as well as talent. In general, it's best not to pick luxury-type activities such as great outdoor trips, hiking in Nepal, or exotic world travel. Though hiking and white-water rafting trips are certainly fun, they mostly show that your family had the money and the resources to send you on this kind of trip, playing right into the hands of biased admissions officers. Plus, these types of activities don't tell the admissions office much about you except for the fact that you survived the ordeal. Nor is this the right moment to pick the company you started up that brings in lots of cash.

As far as length is concerned, this essay is short (the Common Application recommends 150 words, but you can safely write one-half to three-quarters of a page single spaced with no problem). The best strategy is to pick an activity that holds a personal appeal for you and to describe it in detail. The biggest mistake students make is failing to provide specific details. Remember, it's the details that make these essays interesting. Anyone can knock off a few clichéd lines about how their volunteer work at the church on Sunday was their favorite activity because it feels good to help others, but that's sooo boring (and typical). Let's look at a few examples of interesting and detailed descriptions. First is this essay by a student who puts a new twist on political and international relations.

By the third time I was asked to take over a country, I had gotten used to it. Somalia had been tricky, of course, because there were so many warring factions and virtually no government infrastructure. My professor at the foreign policy program helped me along in this simulation, explaining which regions were most volatile and which areas the Special Forces ought to steer clear of altogether. When I invaded Israel as the Egyptian minister of defense at a Model UN conference, I didn't need to take it over per se—just put the squeeze on Sharon to release the hostages. And so, with two fake campaigns under my belt, I figured that my January 2003 assignment in international relations class to invade Iraq as the United States would be fairly simple. Unfortunately, it was.

In simulations such as these, war, conflict, bargaining, and diplomacy simply cannot be reproduced in the same context as the high stakes of modern international relations. I realized while watching CNN in March that invading Iraq was not quite as easy as depicted in my PowerPoint presentation. It lacked the real people, the real property, and the real pressure that real statesmen and real citizens felt. And for a moment, I felt a little angry that I had spent so much time studying the ideas of foreign policy and not the realities. I had read books by Thomas Friedman, papers by Hans Morgenthau, articles by Samantha Power, and interviews by Jimmy Carter. I had written papers expounding on theories for conduct of the United States in a globalized world, studied the war strategies of Machiavelli, Sun Tzu, and Kissinger, and studied the lives of almost all the American secretaries of state. I read Robert Kagan's *Of Paradise and Power*, John Gaddis's analysis of Bush's national security strategy, and Walter Russell Meade's *Special Providence* and incorporated their ideas into my own worldview. I loved ideas, but how could I reconcile them with reality?

I found a personal solution one day when my teacher, during a lecture, rhetorically posed the eternal question: Are you an idealist or a realist? I had never been able to resolve this question. Did I believe that reality was unchangeable and all-encompassing, or did I believe it could be remade according to certain ideals? Ambivalence gave way to the feeling that this was a false dilemma. Why couldn't ideas reflect reality, and why could reality not be affected by ideas? My ideas of military strategy had failed to reflect the realities of war, but perhaps the fourth time I am instructed to embark on a military campaign my ideas will become incrementally more wedded to reality. To me, this defines the process of education itself, the process by which the mind studies the ideal, theoretical world and translates it into a workable reality.

First of all, what a great opening sentence—catchy, funny, and totally original. Notice how the student *shows* (through vivid use of historical example) rather than simply *tells* the reader about his interest in diplomacy. By telling briefly about his independent readings, he gets across his sense of initiative by talking about many well-regarded books he studied on his own. Finally, in the last paragraph, he actually presents a very sophisticated point of view that shows a strong understanding of how diplomacy really works. Even in a brief essay, he does not oversimplify.

In the next example, a student chooses to focus on her commitment to scientific research, a thread that runs throughout her entire essay.

Sure you can talk the talk, but can you walk the walk? School teaches us worthwhile concepts, but it can't prepare us completely for life. We learn to understand the results of work done by people in the real world, and to communicate with others. In essence we learn to talk the talk. But that isn't enough. Somewhere in between graduating from high school and achieving success in a fulfilling job, we need to learn how to apply these tools, and what ideas and concepts to use in the process. Then we need to do something concrete—

we need to walk the walk. That's why I spend so much of my free time in labs. Research is something I love, something I can picture myself doing for the rest of my life. There is nothing like the thrill of having your experiment work or seeing the structure of a diamond under the microscope to light the fire under a young researcher. But simply being a researcher isn't enough for me. I need to feel my research has the potential to have an impact on the way people live. I have no illusions that my high school research will be groundbreaking; after all, I'm a bit young for a Nobel prize. My aim is to start putting to work the body of information I acquired in high school so that I can apply my knowledge to major scientific research. All my various research projects (detailed on my activity list) take me a little closer to that goal.

This student was a powerhouse researcher. Unlike other students who may complete one summer program during the four years of high school, this student had spent six to eight weeks every summer since eighth grade doing research at prominent national labs. Many of her projects turned into published papers on interesting research topics. A professor she worked with took the time to write an incredible recommendation that emphasized how impressive she was. He said she was the only high school student ever to work in the lab, a notable accomplishment for a young person. Though the writer uses a serious tone, there are some lighter moments of self-deprecating humor (that she hasn't won the Nobel prize yet) that let us see a bit of an impish personality. Finally, the student emphasizes the importance of the activity not only to her but also to future beneficiaries of the research discoveries, which centered on Lyme disease, an illness that affects many.

Finally, let's look at another interesting description that focuses on a less than typical activity:

I'm an art museum addict. In the past year, I've visited the Hermitage, the British Museum, and the National Gallery. When a Van Gogh exhibition came to town this spring, I couldn't wait to see it. While in London I saw a Pissarro exhibit, and while in Minneapolis, I caught an exhibition of early Romantic painters at the Minneapolis Institute of Arts. I have a soft spot for Van Gogh and Degas in particular. Van Gogh's impressionist style and vivid colors express his emotions in a way I can relate to on an artistic front. Degas's favorite subject, ballet dancers, has always been of interest to me since I was a ballerina for ten years.

My love of these two artists led me to capture the best of each one's techniques on one canvas. First I did studies of their artwork, mimicking Van Gogh's brushstrokes and studying the way Degas made a studio scene look as if it were in motion. Then I began my fusion of their works. I first created the background, knowing that it would set the mood for the piece. I applied the paint in abstract, harsh brushstrokes, blending the colors so that they melded into a coherent whole that gave off a sense of movement. Next I put in the ballerina. As I painted her, I remembered my intensive study of ballet, and carefully chose her pose. In my painting, she seems to be caught in the middle of a movement, glancing in the direction of her arm, watching her movements carefully. She represents a fusion of two of my favorite artists, as well as one of my favorite arts.

While I never know exactly what my piece will look like when I'm through, half the fun is waiting to see how it will turn out. Sometimes I imagine something as realistic, but it becomes an impression of the subject instead of a true representation. I may start out with only a vague idea of what I want something to become, but as I begin to sketch and paint, details find their way onto the canvas, making an image of the imprint in my head. The freedom that art allows me is what draws me back piece after piece. Faces come alive through paint and pastels; landscapes sway with the wind through watercolor and colored pencil.

What makes this essay interesting are the details and the behind-the-scenes process of creating a work of art. The student avoids the clichéd approach of just stating "I really enjoy painting" and instead gives us a glimpse of the process of artistic creation. A short but elegant piece.

Summary

This essay should be short and vivid. You should focus on something that is a major commitment. Try to pick something that will be reinforced in other parts of the application. Avoid clichés, luxury travel, flat descriptions, and dull writing. This is not the time to be general—give examples that show how much you love this activity. Feel free to explain anything that will not be obvious to a general reader, perhaps an unusual hobby or an unconventional activity. Above all, let your passion shine through.

3

THE WARM-UP ESSAY REDUX

MOST MEANINGFUL INTELLECTUAL EXPERIENCE

Why should you bother writing an extra 250-word essay on your most meaningful intellectual experience if the Common Application doesn't even specifically ask for it? There are at least four good reasons: (1) It's hard enough to communicate all your interests in the compressed format of the application, so this kind of essay adds another dimension to your profile. (2) Because you will be judged roughly 70 percent on your academic profile and only 25 to 30 percent on your extracurricular activities, it's a good idea to empha- size your academic strengths. (3) This essay can easily be adapted into the most common supplemental question found on applications, "Tell us why you want to go to X school."

(4) As the title of the chapter indicates, this is a good warm-up for the major essays.

By now you should be seeing a trend regarding what admissions officers are looking for: passion and depth of involvement. This is the time to focus on a subject or academic area you love, not necessarily one that you are good at. Just because you are a math whiz doesn't mean that you love math. You are not limited to a school topic. If you love astronomy and have spent years memorizing the stars, spotting Messier objects in your telescope, and attending star parties with your local astronomy club, you could certainly pick astronomy and describe your interest, even if you never took a formal class. Because most students write utterly boring and banal essays ("I like math because it has definite answers in black and white and is easy for me"), it will work to your advantage to think long and hard so you can choose a subject area that really fascinates you.

Here's an idea—try to think back to any major research papers you wrote in high school. Even if math really isn't your cup of tea, you could certainly focus on a narrow area such as the research paper you did on Archimedes's method of exhaustion (I'm not making this up—I actually did write a ten-page research paper on this Greek mathematician's method of measuring the area under a curve well before calculus was discovered.). Have you done any experiments, research, or out-of-school projects that reflect a major interest? Rather than just saying you like English class because you love reading, talk about how you discovered a love of words and books and what types of works you read.

Think passion and intellectual depth. If there is one single area that admissions officers are looking for above all others, it is *intellectual firepower*. Though there are many valedictorians (one from every high school graduating in the country, if you stop to think about it), there are few who show a deep and sincere love of learning. Those few are the ones who are accepted most often into the most selective colleges. I think it's easier to see what I'm talking about through some concrete examples taken from my former students.

I glanced up at my opponent over the ancient board decorated with black and white stones arranged in woven lines and swirls, patterns that had just spelled my defeat. Offering my hand and a smile, I spoke for the first time in an hour.

"I resign. Thank you for the game."

I first became acquainted with the game of Go around age twelve. In the middle of a busy mall whose main attractions were movies, clothing, and candy, I frequented an inconspicuous corner shop that dealt in puzzles and games. That day, however, I noticed a small magnetic Go set resting on a shelf in the back. As a Chinese youngster, I had of course heard of the game. Go has had a long time to build up its reputation—three thousand years, in fact. I pestered my dad to buy it along with a booklet on the game. On that first evening—and many evenings thereafter—I spent hours poring over that booklet. Later, I acquired several more books specific to all different aspects of the game—the opening, attack and defense, life and death, invasion—devouring them with equal enthusiasm. At the same time, I searched for opponents to practice against. During the summer after my freshman year, I discovered the Kisedo Go server and promptly created an account for myself so that I could play online. I improved rapidly.

From the moment I joined the Go club at my high school, I became the official tutor for newcomers and beginners. I gave teaching games and clarified points of strategy. Although by no means an expert or even an exceptionally strong player, I was also able to produce a strategy guide to the game suitable for beginners who had just learned the rules. Now, as the president of the Go club, I am working to spread knowledge of this underrecognized game (at least in this country), beginning with my own high school.

Unlike chess, its nearest comparison in international recognition and depth, Go is primarily a game of construction in which pieces are added, rather than a game of destruction in which pieces are removed. The board begins entirely empty, a blank canvas ready to be shaped into a work of art by the interplay between black and white, yin and yang. It is a game of surrounding that unfolds as a large-scale territorial war punctuated by numerous distinct battles. The winner is the player who, at the end, controls the majority of the land.

In many ways, the contrast between Go and chess is reflective of the differences between Eastern and Western culture and warfare. Battles are fought over territory, rather than aiming at the checkmating of the opposing general or king. Stones are played on the intersections of the board, signifying intersections of key routes, rather than the empty spaces in the open battlefields of chess. Go strategy is peppered with seemingly vague terms such as "shape," "taste," "thickness," and "heaviness," in contrast to the more tangible "forks" and "skewers" of chess. This is akin to the contrast between the currents of Eastern mysticism and the logic of Western science. To master the game of Go, one must be attuned to the ebbs and the flows of the game and be able to balance the subtle flavors in the shape, influence, and potential of each stone. A strong Go player is as much an artist and a philosopher as a master strategist. For an aspiring player like me, Go is an aesthetic ideal worth pursuing for its own sake.

This is just a superb essay on all fronts. I love essays where you learn something new—it makes reading applications exciting and interesting for the poor admissions officer stuck at home trying to slog through thirty files a day. The student clearly shows a love of intellectual pursuits. Plus, there are not scores of applicants who are accomplished Go players, so this essay definitely helps the student stand out. Finally, the student does an excellent job getting across the nuances of the game rather than just saying how good a player he is. Even though it's a tad long, it's a top-notch essay.

I mentioned in the beginning of the chapter that this essay on your most meaningful intellectual experience can easily be morphed into a "Why do you want to attend our school?" essay with the simple addition of a few lines. Let's look at how the following student transformed hers into such an essay:

I have always been an American history buff. In fourth grade I remember the chill that ran down my spine when I sat in Ford's Theater during a class trip. I had just read about how John Wilkes Booth ran up to the balcony (the very one I gazed at from below) and assassinated President Lincoln. Suddenly history was more than a textbook reading assignment. In eighth grade, my social studies teacher held a mock trial. I was assigned to defend Colonel John Chivington for his role in the Sand Creek Massacre of 1864. Although history had proven him guilty, I successfully convinced my classmates to acquit the colonel.

In advanced placement American history, our class

began with excerpts from Jared Diamond's *Guns, Germs and Steel: The Fates of Human Societies* and Joseph Ellis' *Founding Brothers*. I found the reading so interesting that I bought copies of both books and continued to read them outside of class. History is exciting to me because it brings into sharp focus the important trends and patterns of the past. Another of my favorite American-history-related texts is Work X by Professor S, a professor at your college. In this book, he explores the life of Amos Webber, an African American janitor who helped fugitive slaves achieve freedom on the Underground Railroad. Reading about other professors and their unconventional perspectives on our nation's history is one of my hobbies. Take the example of Professor H, who on the first day of classes at School Y removes the students' book bags. When students ask what happened to their belongings, Professor H responds by saying, "I discovered them in the same way Columbus discovered America, by claiming to discover something that already belonged to someone else." I got a taste of the enthusiasm and expertise of School Z's professors when I took a government course taught by Professor J, chair of the Department of Government. This is the caliber of classes I look forward to at your college.

This student sounds intellectual. Why? First of all, she is extremely well read and integrates several relevant books into her discussion of history. Second, she avoids the cliché that 90 percent of students who pick history use: "Those who cannot remember the past are condemned to repeat it." The use of this much overused Santayana quote elicits an instant feeling of repugnance and horror—*never* mention this quote or any other overused clichés about history. She even cites a professor from that particular college, which shows initiative and her real interest in the school. I love her opening lines about how her childhood interest in history was so vivid that it still evokes chills. The essay shows some real thought and depth, and in only about four hundred words, that is no mean feat.

Lastly, let's take a look at a very well-written essay on German-language study.

The German language has been part of my life since third grade. At first, studying a foreign language seemed neat because it served as a secret code of sorts, hiding our conversations from non-German-speakers. As I grew older and learned more about the language, I became interested in the grammar, syntax, and verb structure.

As a mathematically inclined thinker, I thrived in my German lessons when I was asked to conjugate a verb or learn different tenses. The patterns that the words and forms fit into made it easy for me to memorize a new grammatical topic. Also, once I learned sentence structure, composing a sentence was similar to plugging variables into an equation. The sequential learning involved in math (starting with simple topics and applying those simple things to more complex topics) is also very prominent in learning a foreign language. Before I could learn the past tense, I had to be sure I knew how to conjugate verbs in the present tense. I also had to memorize the gender (masculine, feminine, or neuter) of nouns before I moved on to learning declensions of adjectives and cases.

Another component in my German studies was learning the difference between German and English word usage. In German, the perfect and simple past tenses have different connotations than they do in English. For example, in English we use the simple past tense in normal conversation to say, "I said." The simple past in German is rarely used when speaking. It is more frequently found in a third-person narrative in which the events are in the distant past. The simple past can also be used, though it is uncommon, to describe something that happened recently but is still true. In English, a person can say, "That is what I said," and mean either that it is still true or that it is now false. The perfect past tense in German is the tense used to describe something from the recent past that is not necessarily still true. German speakers use the perfect past almost exclusively in their everyday conversations.

Starting German at an early age made it a lot easier

for me to grasp the language quickly. Surprisingly, it also helped me learn English grammar. I learned about direct and indirect objects in German before my English teachers began teaching it in school. By the time I was required to diagram sentences for my English classes, I was already well aware of cases and parts of speech. Learning German cases also cemented the knowledge of when to use "who" or "whom" in a sentence. This aspect of learning a language, although small and seemingly insignificant, contributes to my overall love for foreign languages and has helped me realize language as an ongoing passion.

The student who wrote this essay focused more on her math, science, and engineering interests in her other essays, so this essay served the purpose of getting across another one of her major interests: German. Though this essay is not overly complicated, the student provides the reader with enough interesting examples to put some muscle behind her words. It's easy to see how with a few sentences added to the end of the essay, she could tie in her interests in math, German, and engineering in a strong "why" paragraph (as in why you are a good match for the school and why you were attracted to the school in the first place).

Summary

1. Be brief, vivid, and to the point.

2. Give as many details as you can.

3. If you've done any interesting research projects, be sure to mention them.

4. Avoid all clichés about the subject.

5. Either pick an unusual subject or pick one aspect of a subject so your essay doesn't read like the standard "I love numbers ergo I like math" essay.

6. Before adding some specific sentences about the college's specific department, do some Web research to find out if that department is strong. After all, you don't want to say you look forward to studying engineering at a school that doesn't even have an engineering major. Major faux pas.

7. Don't forget the header with your name, Social Security number, date of birth, and high school name in the upper right-hand corner.

8. Spell-check and proofread.

4

THE MAIN ESSAY

It still amazes me that during the four years I read essays for Dartmouth, more than 80 percent of those I read were just plain bad. It always struck me as odd because we received upward of twelve thousand applications a year from the best and the brightest students in the country. How was it possible to have such a talented applicant pool producing such poor essays? Then it hit me—colleges are asking brilliant and multitalented students to get their whole life down on paper: to fit that life into roughly a single-spaced page of words, 12-point Times New Roman. These are the same students who are used to producing work for a particular purpose: an English essay written expressly for their English teacher, a Spanish composition about Pablo Neruda, or a history paper about the fall of the Roman Empire for an AP history teacher. Yet they are completely lost trying to imagine what the gatekeepers of college admissions offices are looking for. Unfortunately, they usually guess wrong and go for the profound, life-changing essay that just doesn't work for a seventeen-year-old applying to college. As deep as you think you are, philosophical observations coming from a high school senior do not carry the weight you might imagine.

The lesson we learn from the preponderance of weak essays is that it's worth it to stop and think about what you are writing, whom you are writing it for, and why you are writing it. There are lots of college guides that focus entirely on the college essay. Most of them are not very helpful, but a few are worth reading. *On Writing the College Application Essay* by Harry Bauld is a classic. If you want to read a hilarious and practical book on what *not* to write and what you should write, this should be your first choice. Though his book is short, its pithiness is what makes it so funny and so on target. Without naming all his exact categories, I'll say that he breaks down the horribly clichéd essays students write into roughly eight general categories—all of which you should avoid like the plague. The Outward Bound essay (substitute NOLS or any other rigorous outdoor adventure company) in which the student starts with the vivid retelling of the harrowing experience ("My legs trembled as the ten-foot snowdrifts piled up against our tattered shelter . . .") and ends with his inevitable survival is just not going to get any points with the admissions office. Surprise—the student always lives to tell the tale. Or the death-of-a-relative essay in which the student lovingly eulogizes the deceased grandparent—lovely for an English paper, but it does little to tell the admissions office anything about the student himself.

In short, the biggest pitfall students face is that they tend to talk about anything but themselves. The second mistake is talking about themselves in a most impersonal, English-class, third-person way. It's hard to blame students because their English teachers have hammered into them for years that they should not write in the first person. Let's make one thing clear: *Your college essay should be personal and it should be written in the first person.* Period. Margit Dahl, the former director of undergraduate admissions at Yale, listed a few general points that reinforce my thoughts. She says, "Don't be shy . . . be personal," "narrow your focus," "be unusual," "convey your curiosity," and "consider your audience."*

Don't be shy. This is not the time for students to be detached—this essay should come straight from the heart and take the admissions officer right into your life. How does your voice sound? How are you different from other students?

Narrow your focus. Your eight-week summer travels across Europe cannot be captured in a 500-word essay. Pick one incident or an interesting encounter that made you think hard about something.

The Bottom Line Year Book 2002, Boardroom Books, Division of Boardroom Reports, Inc, Greenwich, Connecticut, pp. 306–7.

Be unusual. Find the extraordinary in the ordinary, to paraphrase Dahl. Take an everyday incident and pick one aspect that was truly earth-shattering.

Convey your curiosity. Remember that above all, admissions officers are looking for intellectual curiosity. Well, here is your chance to show it. Get excited, trace an intellectual interest, recount a hobby or fascination with something.

Consider your audience. Admissions officers in the height of admissions season read for six to eight hours a day (up to thirty files a day) for three to four months on end. They are tired, they are bored, and they are trying to get through the day's reading. This is the time to stand out, not to blend in with the pack and put your audience to sleep.

One literary technique that may help is what I have taught to my English students for years—Hemingway's show-not-tell style of writing. Remember *The Sun Also Rises*? There is a classic Hemingway moment toward the end of the novel when Jake, the main character, has let Montoya (the hotel proprietor and friend of the bullfighter Romero) down by corrupting the young Romero with drink and by setting him up with Brett, a femme fatale. The only way the reader can sense how Montoya feels at all is by reading a three-word sentence. When Jake enters the room, Hemingway simply writes of Montoya, "He looked down." That simple gesture says it all. The disappointment, the corruption of the most pure thing, raw *afición*, by someone Montoya had trusted for years. The careless reader would skip right over this line and might later wonder how others reacted to Romero's decline. It would have been so much less powerful if Hemingway had resorted to what the typical high school student pens: "Montoya was furious—how could Jake fix up Romero with Brett when he knows it will ruin his career?" Yikes!

Taking our cues from Hemingway, there are some general writing points to keep in mind:

1. Eliminate almost every adjective and adverb—high school students rely too much on these crutches. Notice how great writers rely on sharp description and spare dialogue rather than on adjectival lists.

2. Avoid the typical high school clichéd topics: the adventure travel essay, the community service "I helped save the world" essay, the "I dived and caught the ball and we won the game" essay, et cetera.

3. Focus on one small incident and expand it into an essay.

4. Be personal, not impersonal.

5. Write in the first person.

6. If you don't have to use the weak connector "and," don't. Students love "I studied all night for the test and I got an A" when they should be using a causal relationship: "Because I studied . . . I got an A." Lose the "and."

7. Make sure when you're done to spell-check and proofread your essay. Have a friend look it over carefully as well.

8. Don't overedit or use thesaurus words—keep it simple. Those ten-thousand-dollar words always stand out like a jelly doughnut among the chocolate crèmes. "I read a plethora of books." Ick!

9. Don't tackle a huge political or philosophical topic that you can't possibly cover in a short essay.

10. Avoid pretentious diction.

11. Be as specific as you can when recounting events. Give the reader that you-are-there feeling—be vivid!

12. Write about something that is meaningful and interesting to you. If it puts you to sleep, you can imagine what it's doing to the admissions officers.

Now that we've seen what *not* to write, what *should* you write? The best essays take one small slice of life and expand ~thing meaningful. Is there any incident that are? Any early childhood indications of a talent in your life that was to become a central passion? Any intellectual experiences that really turned you on to a particular topic or area of study? Another activity you can try is to focus on one small aspect of something you love. One art student spent a page describing the process of drawing a line on paper. The reader learned what she thought about how her eyes perceived her surroundings and how she created art. The best way to visualize what I'm talking about is to look at the following examples written by some of my former clients.

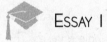 ## ESSAY 1

I first became interested in Latin in seventh grade thanks to an extraordinary teacher. I had no idea what to expect on my first day of junior high school when I walked into my Latin class. From my vantage point at the back of Room 43, I could barely make out the teacher over a sea of high schoolers' heads. For our first night's homework, Ms. C. assigned us to translate a short Latin passage, *"Servus in horto est."* It was easy going at first; I was happy just to be able to understand the meaning, "The slave is in the garden." I did not think much beyond the actual words. I had yet to learn about conjugations, meter, subjunctive, and declensions, which would explain, among other things, why *horto* was the correct form instead of *hortus.* Propelled by an incredibly inspiring teacher, I began my long journey down the road to learning the dynamics and art of translating and reading Latin.

The complicated grammar and syntax of Latin gives it the power to convey meaning that English struggles to convey, even with its immensely rich vocabulary. The power of the English language derives largely from picking the one perfect word out of ten possible choices that mean almost the same thing. In Latin, it is syntax and grammar that hold the power. One of the things that I love about Latin is that it presents the reader with a struggle. For example, a reader of Latin might wonder, why did the author use a strange syntactical form? How does this line sound when read aloud and how does the oral component change the meaning? How does one translate the ablative absolute? Latin is mysterious, leaving thousands of translators toiling over their translations of even single phrases. The famous opening lines of *The Aeneid* are translated in three completely different ways by three famous translators. Fitzgerald: "I sing of warfare and a man at war"; Mandelbaum: "I sing of arms and of a man"; Dickinson: "Of arms I sing and the hero." As you can see, different translators emphasize different things. Fitzgerald takes greater liberties, emphasizing war over the individual hero. Mandelbaum translates literally, emphasizing one man, Aeneas. Dickinson emphasizes Aeneas as heroic, more than just a man.

To illustrate the expansiveness of Latin syntax, I will use the ablative absolute, a construction that is easy to recognize because it involves just two adjacent words in the ablative case. When translating the ablative absolute into English, the reader must infer the meaning from the author's tone and the context of the rest of the passage. The ablative absolute is independent of the main clause grammatically, but it is connected to the rest of the sentence as it explains circumstances. The fun part is that the two words—in this case, "dog" and "fed," both in the ablative case with no verbs or adverbs—can be used to explain circumstance ("the dog having been fed"), time ("once the dog was fed"), cause ("since the dog was fed"), or concession ("although the dog was fed"). The reader's only resource is the context. This ambiguity is what makes Latin so beautiful and rewarding. It is up to the reader to figure out what the author means. Understanding this challenge has taught me how to make the most of reading English. In Shakespeare's works, I listen to the sounds and the meter as I do in Latin, and ascribe new meanings. In Milton's *Paradise Lost* I was excited to find striking similarities between Milton's style and Virgil's in *The Aeneid*. It is the anomalies in the writing and the disruptions in the meter that make a passage interesting. In other words, when the author chooses to deviate from his rhyme scheme (in Virgil, dactylic hexameter), the reader must take note. A well-chosen spondaic substitution for a dactyl carries all kinds of implications for interpretation.

I remember translating a passage in Book IV of *The Aeneid*, a book that revolves around the tragic love story between Dido and Aeneas. Aeneas falls in love with Dido but is forced to leave her to carry out his destiny to found Rome. Dido, in despair, commits suicide. When I first read the following passage from Book IV, I was not able to extract the meaning,

Ergo Iris croceis per caelum roscida pennis,
Mille trahens varios adverso sole colores, devolat . . .

(4. 700–701)

The literal translation of these lines is "Therefore the dewy Iris flies down through the sky on saffron-colored wings, dragging a thousand different colors across from the sun." At first, I was stumped because I did not know what "a thousand different colors" would have to do with the rest of this sentence about Iris traveling down to release Dido's soul from her dead corpse. When I read the passage a second time, I realized that as Iris was flying down from the heavens, she was drawing a *rainbow* through the sky by dragging "a thousand different colors across from the sun." The beauty of this word picture seemed even more striking after struggling to interpret it. After scanning the meter of the rainbow line, I found that the meter is made up primarily of dactyls (one long syllable followed by two short syllables) instead of two long, harsh syllables (a spondee). Virgil chose to adhere to strict dactylic hexameter in order to create a light, fluid rhythm that fits the context of a rainbow fluttering through the sky.

After taking four years of Latin (as far as my high school would take me), I decided that I did not want to quit. I contacted a professor at X college who teaches ancient Greek as well as Latin at a high school in another part of the city. After reading *The Odyssey* in English, I wanted to be able to read epics such as *The Odyssey* in their original form. I began meeting with my new teacher, Mr. F., to continue reading Latin, and to begin learning ancient Greek. It has been two years since I started learning Greek, and I love it just as much as Latin, but in different ways. Greek is more complex grammatically, which gives it more flexibility in its use of language. Greek has an active, middle, and passive voice, while Latin has just active and passive. Greek verbs have six principal parts, while Latin verbs have only four. Greek also has a more flexible syntax, which allows a wider variety of expression. Greek is more of a struggle, but it still gives me the same joy of translating that Latin does. One time, a passage of Aristophanes had me and my professor laughing, because in *The Wasps,* Aristophanes casts a cheese grater, a cooking pot, and all the furniture as witnesses to a court case, and then has the prosecutor pretend to listen to the cheese grater's testimony. Being able to enjoy the humor in a satire that was written around 420 B.C. is quite an experience.

When I visited X college last spring, I sat in on a Latin class and a Greek class. During my second visit this fall, I attended another Latin class. I made a point to visit these classes because I plan to pursue my interest in the classics at a school with a strong department. I know that at X I can continue my studies in the classics, while also pursuing one or two modern languages, along with my other areas of interest, including literature and chemistry.

I'll admit my bias because I'm somewhat of an armchair classicist myself. But even someone with no classical background would have no problem seeing the intellectual curiosity and passion this student has for classical languages. Notice how specific she is, providing detailed passages, interpretations, and her own struggles with translating. Rather than focusing on the whole of Latin grammar, she zooms in on a construction difficult for many students, the ablative absolute. Her essay is very intellectual, very polished, but also very sincere and straightforward. She avoids using complicated vocabulary, extra adjectives and adverbs, and long sentences. She also manages to make reference to why she wants to attend that particular school, which happens to have a great classics department. Finally, she shows her initiative by seeking out classes in a nearby college because her high school did not offer Greek. Not only did the admissions office love this essay (she was admitted to a prestigious liberal arts college), they offered her a special academic scholarship in the classics, singling out her essay as the deciding factor. Plus, her high school teachers commented on her scholarly talents in classical languages in her recommendations.

ESSAY 2

In psychology, we studied different types of stress. One example is life-changing stress, an event that changes your life dramatically. Examples are the death of a parent or sibling or moving away from home. I experienced a life-changing stressor on September 11, 2001, a day that changed the nation, the world, and my own life. On that day, my father died in the first World Trade Center tower. Losing a parent is difficult at any time of one's life, but to lose one so early is infinitely worse. My father was a senior computer programmer at Cantor Fitzgerald. He was the first to help me learn math. When I was three years old, I had an obsession with watching trains as they rolled by. Every day, my father would take me out to the train station and I would watch the trains pass. He introduced me to math by teaching me how to count the cars on the trains. I spent endless hours of my childhood counting the train cars as they passed by, in both English and Chinese. When my father died, my life was changed forever. As my mother always reminds me, I have been entrusted with new responsibilities as the "man of the house"— mundane things at first, such as taking out the garbage or watching my brother when my mom comes home late from work. But these jobs grew with time: I now drive my brother to piano lessons, take airplane trips by myself to faraway summer activities, and even handle my own tax return.

Before 9/11, I was a typical introverted, nerdy Asian student. I was somewhat antisocial and had few friends. Academically, I did not stand out from my peers. At first after my father's death, I was even more withdrawn for a time, but that changed after I was accepted into a summer program called CTY (Center for Talented Youth) after scoring high in the Johns Hopkins Talent Search.

When I first heard I was going to spend three weeks of my summer away from home, living with an unknown roommate and five hundred other unknown people, and spend seven hours of the already short twenty-four-hour day taking Algebra I, I was horrified. How could I spend that much time away from home and with no one I knew? What would my brother do without either his dad or his brother to help him? Once I got there, I discovered integrating with everyone else was not as difficult as it seemed. Everyone else was in the same boat and wanted to make new friends. The math teacher, Mr. Q., and his TA, Amy C., made the algebra course exciting. When I was working hard with my fellow classmates, I began to forget how far I was from home and started to immerse myself in math. I learned how to factor and manipulate numbers. My ability, confidence, and interest in using mathematics dramatically increased in this short three-week time. On the personal side, I became more social and made new friends who I would meet again at future CTY experiences. We bonded through toiling on the same math tests, playing Frisbee, and a million other small things as simple as cloud watching.

As a result of the summer experience, I became more confident in school, math, and finding new friends. I entered the honor classes in eighth grade and did well in them. Because my father was a computer programmer, he would help me late in the evening when he got home from work—math was one of his strongest areas. Math continued to play a key role in my life. In ninth grade, I took double math courses (Geometry and Algebra II), something no one else in my school attempted. I also tutored a student, Elizabeth, in math that year as part of peer tutoring. I joined clubs where I met new friends who would shape me into the person I am today, a much more open and outgoing person. In activities such as Math Team and the Science Olympiad, I honed my math skills. In weekly practices, we work our way through worksheets of past problems until we can solve them with ease. Though the Science Olympiad is mostly a science competition, I handle the events with a mathematical application. The event called Fermi Questions uses the unusual application of mathematics for estimation. I was asked to find a fast, rough estimate of obscene quantities to answer questions such as "How many drops of water are there in Lake Erie?" It was fun sifting through books looking for facts that gave the most outrageous numbers, such as the fact that it takes 120 million cars bumper to bumper to go from the earth to the moon. Also, I had a chance to apply my mathematics skills to physics in Out and Back, when we had to construct a mousetrap-powered car to travel ten meters forward and then backward without deviating from the course. Through my efforts, I was rewarded with a first-place medal in Out and Back and a fourth-place medal in Fermi Questions.

The summer before junior year, I was hit with another life-changing stressor (granted, on a much smaller scale): changing schools. The transition was a bit turbulent—I had made many friends at my old school, most of whom I still keep in contact with, and had made my mark on many clubs and activities there.

On the bright side, I met someone who dramatically changed my opinion on math and made me consider a future in mathematics—my AP BC Calculus teacher, Mr. I. Unlike my bumbling sophomore Precalculus teacher, who constantly needed to ask other teachers for help when I asked questions, "Dr. I," as we would jokingly call him, possessed an almost alarming knowledge of mathematics and taught without using notes or supplements. He entertained us with his knowledge of star graphs or explained the unsolved Riemann's hypothesis, a theory that if proven would be able to break any computer-encrypted files and earn you one million dollars as part of the Clay Mathematics Institute's Prize Problem (and even more with patents). He used an unusual teaching style that involved the entire class in solving problems. Mr. I. would call up a student to solve a problem. If the student understood how to do the problem, he would explain it to the class on the board. If the student was clueless (which happens frequently in Calculus), the entire class would work together to solve the problem. I thrived in this cooperative environment. Often, I ended up being the key person in solving problems.

His class motivated me to spend extra time at home reading ahead and trying to understand the upcoming topics so I could help the class solve more problems.

This summer, I visited my father's grave, in Taiwan (after his body was recovered we sent it to Taiwan, where he had grown up). His death represented a changing point in my life. Though I would do anything to have him back, in a funny way stepping in to take his place helped me change from an introverted young boy to an extroverted and focused honors student who enjoys learning for its own sake. When I look toward the future and my time in college, I see myself reliving the summer camp experiences of meeting new people and working in a collaborative environment so I can help others along the way. I know in my heart that my father would be proud of my efforts, as he was always the first to lend a hand and help someone else with a difficult concept. In part, I hope to honor his memory through my achievements in college and beyond.

This essay makes me cry every time I read it. It's great because it combines important personal information with academic interests. If the essay had simply dwelled on the student's father's death, it would have elicited sympathy, but it would not have added much to what we know about the student's interests. Plus, the writer shows an introspective streak, poking fun at himself as a "nerdy" Asian student. But then he brings us along on his transformation, both mental and personal, as he discovers his passion for math. The last paragraph is just gorgeous—it's difficult to avoid being maudlin when writing about the death of a parent, but this student managed to avoid clichés. A terrific essay and one of my personal favorites.

 Essay 3

Racing through the hallway, placing a feather into my green felt hat, I dove onto our living room sofa, eager to watch my favorite movie, *Robin Hood*. At the time, I was mesmerized by the outlaw for the same reasons everyone my age was fascinated with superheroes. Robin Hood was dashing, he fought for justice, and most importantly, he could shoot a bow and arrow better than anyone else in Nottingham. For several years after first watching the legendary outlaw's cartoon exploits, I held a special place in my heart for him. I can remember watching that Disney movie countless times and carefully crafting my favorite hat out of green felt so that I could share in the magic of my hero. I begged my parents to take me to the local Renaissance Festival each year so that I could, after an hour and a half of sitting in a car, finally hone my own archery skills. I built castles out of Lego blocks so that my little Lego Robin Hood could rescue a damsel from the dungeon. But soon the magic of Robin Hood began to fade. Action figures and costumes were replaced by basketball and homework. Before long, my trusty green felt hat had been retired too, stuffed carelessly into my toy chest behind my forgotten Etch-A-Sketch and under a pile of stuffed animals. Until last year, I probably would have said that Robin Hood and I had crossed paths for the last time.

It was last December, while reading T. H. White's *The Once and Future King* for junior English, that I was thrown back to my childhood world of knights in shining armor, dragons, and wizards. It wasn't too long before Robin Hood appeared in the book, and my outlaw friend, complete with his band of Merry Men, came waltzing back into my life. When my class was assigned a research paper covering any aspect of the novel, Robin Hood was the man for the job. For the first time, I would come to know Robin Hood from a student's perspective, not just as a wide-eyed four-year-old. My topic: Was Robin Hood real? Despite all the scholarly dissertations and crude blogs written about the outlaw, no one has proved or disproved Robin Hood's existence. So, perhaps with childish enthusiasm, I embarked on a project to find the rugged woodsman I had grown to love as a kid.

I spent the next few days digging through everything from Robin Hood junkie Web pages (I was amazed at the number I found) to the scholarly Robin Hood Project, an extensive study of Robin Hood done at the University of Rochester. After trying to decipher a daunting quantity of information, I found three arguments to support Robin Hood's existence and, to my disappointment, about a hundred times as many arguments to refute it. But, despite the seeming futility, I decided to pursue those three arguments to prove that my childhood hero was more than a Walt Disney fabrication. The deeper I delved into the medieval folklore, however, the deeper my hopes sank. My first argument, based largely on evidence from an English clergyman named Joseph Hunter, revealed a historical "Robert Hood" who lived just ten miles outside of Robin Hood's legendary home of Barnsdale. But no evidence could prove that Robert and Robin were in fact the same person. I then pursued my second argument. Inspired by an article written by Canadian medieval expert Allen Wright, I read of a tomb in Loxley that held a striking resemblance to an earlier drawing of Robin Hood's tomb. But, unfortunately, this argument was little more than speculation. I approached the third argument cautiously, fearing now that it would be impossible to prove Robin Hood's authenticity. But, much to my delight, the argument was promising. In 1936, a man named L. V. D. Owen discovered an entry in the English court records of 1225–1226. The entry read, "Robert Hod, fugitive." Even more telling, the records showed that the man in charge of Robert Hod's capture would have been the Sheriff of Nottingham. Although this Robert Hod could have been the man I was after, there was little evidence to prove that he was anything more than a petty thief, so I advanced no further. I was almost ready to admit defeat and conclude that Robin Hood never actually existed.

Saddened, I threw on my metaphorical green felt hat one last time as I plunged into an online encyclopedia article. As I traced and retraced my steps, still hoping to stumble upon another argument, it finally hit me: Who cares if Robin Hood was real? What did it matter if someone at some time dressed up in green tights and "stole from the rich to give to the poor"? What mattered is that someone cared enough to share that message. Men such as T. H. White and Walt Disney had grasped the importance of justice and charity enough to put it in the form of a character that could be understood by everyone, even a little kid sitting in his living room at the age of four. Looking over the countless Web pages I had printed discussing Robin Hood's existence, I realized how impressive it was that a legend, written hundreds of years ago, was still being discussed at length today, and at the core of that legend was the message of justice. Because of this legend, people across the world know, and have passed on to their kids, the concept of justice. I looked up from my computer chair that night and couldn't help but smile at the impact this man in tights had made on my life. As a kid I fell in love with Robin Hood for his heroic deeds, trusty sidekicks, and, of course, cool green hat. But that passion had come full circle as I now experienced a newfound respect for the legend, not as a childhood superhero, but as a message of justice and compassion that continues to live on, whether Robin Hood actually existed or not.

It's hard not to like this essay for its boyish enthusiasm and original topic. Plus years later I remember many of the great details in this essay, including the green felt hat and the Lego Robin Hood castle. But below the charming story lie the traits of a thinker and researcher, two important areas that admissions officers are always on the lookout for. Overall, when I read essays like this, it makes me want to sit down and have coffee with the student, to meet him and find out more about him, and that's an impressive accomplishment and the sign of an original essay.

Let's look at an essay that focuses on an unusual interest—medieval literature.

 ESSAY 4

While other children grew up hearing about the Big Bad Wolf in the story of the Three Little Pigs, I heard tales of someone called Beowulf. *Beowulf* was one of my grandfather's favorite stories, and he felt the need to pass on the fun to me at a very early stage. Maybe he was interested in the battle scenes, the use of alliteration, or the syntax of the poetry. Who knows? When I studied the epic at a more mature time in my life, it took one small word out of the entire archaic text to make it actually mean something to me. And that word would be (drum roll, please) "aglaecwif." Not commonly used today, this was the Old English way of expressing a woman of the Cruella de Vil disposition. Back in the day, the word serve'd to compound a widespread idea into a simple term. It meant "fearsome woman." It still sends shock waves of indignation down my spine to think that one singular term existed to express such a hateful description of a female. This term is actually featured in the text of *Beowulf.* Isn't it convenient that society should promote a need for this word to exist, which would in turn fit nicely into an epic poem to describe the mother of a monster? "Anonymous" must have thought so when he was penning his epic. I, on the other hand, was stunned to discover that gender inequality had such a concrete representation in the Old English language.

Back to my grandfather; I brought him up because he was into this ancient-language stuff too. In fact, he made a career of it, as an English professor specializing in the Old and Middle varieties. As I dove into my investigation of gender in the early stages of English, I couldn't help thinking of my grandfather wearing a smoking jacket, pipe in hand, sitting in his study, analyzing the same words that I now read. But I was in a miniskirt, pink highlighter in hand.

My grandfather might have been enthused by the theme of glory in *Beowulf,* and based a theory on that premise. After all, he was "man," coming from the Sanskrit word "manu," the term for God. As if men were endowed with otherworldly power and inspiration. Why would my grandfather have thought otherwise, surrounded by the good ol' boys, his male colleagues, at the university? He brought his own set of circumstances into the reading of the epic. Personally, I find that to be the most compelling aspect of early literature—that although the works were created in an alien time period and under foreign conditions, my grandfather and I both were able to extract parts that we could gain insight from. The fact that we drew different interpretations from completely different parts of the poem validates the importance of studying early English literature for me.

I read *Beowulf* as "woman," coming from the Old English "wyf-mon": a fusion of the parts "wyf" for wife and "mon" for man. I am tragically reduced to the wife of man. To me, here's where the interesting part comes in. Early English society was influenced by the language of the time, and language continues to mold our existence. The nature of Old English confined women in their actions and thoughts. I imagine being a woman living during the period of Old English and wanting to give a greater purpose to my life than being the best "huswif" (housewife) that I could be. But alas, I would have been out of luck because there simply was not vocabulary to support the notion of a woman with a career. I wouldn't have even been worth my own pronoun until the period of Middle English rolled around. Personally, I enjoy the freedom to choose whatever job I want. It makes me cringe to think that these options would not have been available to me had I lived during Old English times.

However, considering the slighting of women apparent in Old English opened me up to think about whether language influenced society or the sentiments of the society led to the conditions of the language. Either way, I recognized the importance of looking to ancient works of literature to discover hints about the society that generated them. The language, characterization, and plot of *Beowulf* are all clues in piecing together my perception of early English society.

My other favorite part of the study of early literature is that each reader who comes across a work, despite its old age, is able to connect to a certain part and draw his/her own conclusions. Those conclusions may not have anything to do with the original intent of the art, but I think they are still valuable. To me, the value of *Beowulf* lay in the analysis of gender implications. For instance, when Beowulf fights Grendel's mother the author fails to mention the gender of his adversary, as if a female opponent would seem unworthy. While I was outraged by this point, my grandfather may have glanced past it. We each brought our own perspectives to the table when considering the epic.

I am interested in studying early English literature because of all that I came across when analyzing *Beowulf.* Not only were the actual words of the poem meaningful, but the process of extracting a tiny element of the work to scrutinize made me appreciate the fact that each individual takes something different from the text. Further, I was stunned to witness the way that so much about a culture can be recognized based on minute details of its language. I hope to pursue this field of study, and perhaps someday I shall torture, or rather *captivate,* my grandchildren with special readings of *Beowulf.*

Here it is again: passion and initiative, not to mention humor. I found myself laughing out loud at the "(drum roll, please) 'aglaecwif,' " and " 'Anonymous' must have thought so when he was penning his epic."

This is also another good example of an essay that holds the reader's interest because it teaches us something. Throughout the essay, we got the distinct impression that this student has the potential to be a scholar of Old and Middle English (after all, her grandfather was), and that's not a very common area of academic interest. I love the fact that her sly, almost impish personality comes across. She's the kind of student who clearly demonstrates a love of learning but also manages to weave in many attractive personal qualities as well. Mission accomplished!

Finally, let's look at another artistic essay that also gets across some of the personal factors that influenced this student's high school performance.

 Essay 5

I type furiously, banging my fingers on the keyboard, not stopping when I feel my nails crack and chip. I've done this so many times before but it never gets old. I type like a wild woman—it feels good to put my words on the screen, like something between falling in love and letting go of inhibitions. I keep going; I write and write like it's the only thing keeping me alive. I write as though I'm three lines away from the Nobel prize.

With a confident *click, click, clack* on the keys I put the finishing touches on my work. I sigh with satisfaction, lean back in my chair, and close my eyes. Best feeling in the world, this is the best feeling in the world. I like to call myself a poetess. After all, poetry is my life.

I first began to dabble in writing when I was in seventh grade. I had an amazing writing teacher who introduced me to the world of free verse. Before that year I had always thought that poems needed to be in strict form, with tight rhymes and a twinkle-twinkle-little-star beat. I never imagined poetry would appeal to me. I'll admit I didn't take to it immediately. My first attempts were all pretty much the same drab love poems about unaffectionate twelve-year-olds. It seemed I was writing just for the sake of writing.

When I reached ninth grade I still hovered on the edge of poetry, not focusing on anything in depth. But then a friend of mine told me about how much she had enjoyed reading Sylvia Plath's *The Bell Jar.*

I borrowed the book from my school's library; from the moment I opened it I was hooked. I couldn't put it down. At several points during my reading I would stop where I was, mark the page, and start writing. Sylvia Plath brought so many emotions out in me, I felt I had to write or I would lose the impulse.

When my mother's behavior grew physically and emotionally abusive, I was forced to leave home right before the beginning of high school. I thought I would never get over how shaken I was. My entire world had fallen apart. Though I felt physically safe in my father's house, I was still very insecure and broken up on the inside. I went into a depression, which few people acknowledged, and therefore I went untreated. When I began to read the tragic poetry of Sylvia Plath I realized that she was suffering and feeling just as scared and empty as I was. For once I didn't feel so alone. Writing my poems as extensions to her prose made me feel like I was a part of something, like I was worth something.

But even after that year I was still a troubled individual. I went through a bad breakup at the end of tenth grade—given my emotional instability, I spiraled back into my depression. I stopped spending time with friends; I stopped going outside; I spent all my time at home questioning what was wrong with me. As a result, upon returning to school I let my grades slip through my fingers. I couldn't handle the feeling of weakness that followed me. Then a new friend came into my life, a poet. After he read some of my poems he told me it would be a shame to give up on everything when I had talent. I took his advice and resumed writing. I posted poems on the Internet, submitted my work to literary magazines, and even went to poetry readings. It felt so good to get my voice out there again. When I felt secure enough to look at what I'd been feeling in the past more objectively, I felt the need to seek help. I started going to therapy and was put on some low-dosage medications. Now I feel that I can thank my poetry for my current state of stability.

Writing isn't the kind of thing I force myself into anymore. I don't go looking for things to be inspired by. Inspiration just finds me. It doesn't matter where I am at the time or what I'm doing; sometimes I just need to write. When I feel like this I sit down (I can't write standing up, it just feels too forced) and I write down all my thoughts. I carry a journal with me all the time and lots of different colored pens and pencils to suit the mood I'm in when I'm inspired.

I believe all my hard work finally paid off when I signed up for a poetry slam. I went there originally just to see a friend of mine read. I brought my journal with me so I could show him some of the works I was most proud of. But at the last moment he put my name on the list. I didn't protest too much (I think that I secretly wanted to read anyway), and when they called my name I solemnly stepped onto the stage, journal in hand.

I found myself staring deep into the abyss. The lights resembled an interrogation room. I had never before seen a microphone look so un-welcoming. It had looked so easy from my chair, five rows short of the back door; what was the difference now? I looked down at my fancy holiday present, a notebook. I remembered copying these words from where I had scrawled them in my class notes. I remembered trying to get my handwriting just right. I remembered there was still a roomful of people staring at me. I took a deep breath and I spoke.

Depth
I am at the depths of what exactly?
Bottom-dwelling masochism
Definition of comprehension

Suddenly, as though they had a mind of their own, my fingers be-gan ticking off the rhythm of my words on my left thigh.

I don't hold on to the appeal of this universal melancholy
Are you only as deep as your river of tears?
Or as profound as the multitudes you feel superior to?

The words tasted good in my mouth and I exhaled them like the last touches on a sweet good-bye kiss.

Or perhaps as intense as the number of
insignificant details you can dwell on or the size
of the bigger picture you claim to see?

Then I felt my shoulders loosen a little and relax themselves. I felt the cool air drying up my sweating palms. I even smiled a little.

A competition of depths is a comparison of colors
Supremacy is a battle over sand
Who really wins in the end?
Tell me,
Tell me I'm not deep enough to understand

I said the rest of the words slowly, adding emphasis when necessary. I smiled, I laughed, I flirted with the audience from my place high above the crowd. I felt beautiful and wonderful. I felt like they all loved and accepted me as a poet. And in that moment I knew I had found my calling.

This is one of my favorites because it really captures how unusual this student is. It also addresses some personal problems that had a detrimental effect on her high school performance. Though she didn't dwell on her C average in high school, she was smart to address her low grades in her essay by alluding to the abuse she endured and the move to her father's house. Her poetic sensibility is apparent throughout the essay as she traces her interest in poetry and how it helped her overcome her depression and get back on track. This student was clearly a high-risk applicant because of her low grades, but this essay did an excellent job of bringing out her intellectual qualities and her potential for success.

Your job in the main essay is to focus on one small aspect of your life and expand it into an essay. It should give some insight into what you are like as a person, how you think, how you approach problems, and what you are interested in. It should communicate passion and a sense of initiative. This is your main chance to impress the admissions committee and to make your presence known. It is not the time to hide behind barriers and write an impersonal essay. Think in-your-face personal—what is it about you that you want the admissions committee to know and understand? Be sure to write about something significant to you—if it's not interesting to you, it sure as heck won't be any more interesting to the admissions committee. If there are any extenuating personal circumstances, definitely mention them, but don't fall into the common trap of making excuses for poor performance. Lots of other students survived their parents' divorce without letting their grades drop. Be vivid, be creative, be interesting—be yourself and let your own personality shine through.

5

THE SUPPLEMENTAL ESSAY

Why write an extra essay if not all colleges ask for one? The simple answer is, why not? Even though the Common Application requires only one main essay, many of the colleges that use the Common Application ask for supplementary information, and usually that means an extra essay. If you're not sure what a particular college requires, go to www.commonapp.org and look up the college's requirements. All the supplemental information will be provided here. Normally the topic is wide open: *Feel free to tell us anything about you that would help us get to know you better.* What should you write about here?

Some perspective is necessary. You want to ask yourself, "What is it about me that I have not been able to communicate to the admissions office so far that reflects who I am?" This is a good time to sit down and read over your activity list, your two smaller essays, your main essay, and part one of your application. Admissions officers are not mind readers. If you don't tell them about a special talent or area of interest, they won't find out about it unless one of your teachers specifically mentions it.

This is the time to be a bit unconventional—write about something you feel passionate about. Write about a personal aspect of yourself that influences how you act day to day. Talk about a movie or book that changed your perspective on life, or an unusual talent you haven't had the chance to bring up. You want to look inward to your very essence. Pretend you are speaking directly to an admissions officer—what piece of the puzzle have you left out of your application?

For students who have had tremendous personal difficulties, this is often a good time to discuss them. I wouldn't devote the main essay to a personal problem because it comes across as too whiny or just as an excuse for poor performance. But this essay is not even required by many schools—use it to explain a situation that would not be evident from your file.

The most important point I'd like to emphasize is that this essay should be *personal*, even more so than the other parts of the application. Let your voice shine through, write clearly, write expressively, write with emotion. Bring out another dimension of your personality that is central to being you. As far as length is concerned, if the main essay is roughly a page and a half single-spaced, this one is closer to one page single-spaced, not much more.

For applications that specifically ask for an extra essay,

follow the same format as the main essay: type the college's name on top, include a header with your name, Social Security number, date of birth, and high school name, and then type the question number of the supplementary question and the question itself.

For those applications that don't ask for any additional information, include it anyway. Admissions officers are usually glad to find out a bit more about an applicant and won't mind a short essay as long as it doesn't slow them down tremendously. You would be imposing on them if you attached your ten-page term paper, but a short personal essay is welcome and shows you took the initiative to include more information than you were asked to. Rather than typing the question, just write the name of the college, the header, and the title "Supplemental Essay," "Additional Essay," or "Extra Essay." In the order of papers, this would be the last item.

Let's look at some personal essays that served a specific purpose in the overall scheme of the application.

 ESSAY I

Brushing the blond wig out of my eyes, I threw on some aviator sunglasses, checked my fly, and strutted out to "Disco Inferno" in front of five hundred people. Thus began my short-lived modeling career in the first of the day's four Disco Fashion Shows, hosted by the student council. The fashion show is my favorite activity for promoting student council affairs because it rouses the typically apathetic students at my high school. Since everyone in the school watches the fashion show, my runway partner and I labored over our dance moves. We settled on any move that would make an unforgettable impression on the audience. My partner did the old-fashioned John Travolta *Saturday Night Fever* dance moves complete with arm swings and hip shakes, while I broke up his dance by robot-walking him off the stage Michael Jackson style.

Our smooth dance grooves certainly helped to promote Disco Spirit Week. I was able to think up even more outrageous acts for each subsequent show, such as robot karate with mini fighting sequences set to the driving beat of Donna Summer's "Hot Stuff." The next day was Disco Clothes Day, so the school was filled with wigs, sunglasses, dance music, and all the shining polyester clothes you could dream of. Thanks in part to my role in the fashion show I was elected student council parliamentarian.

Once I got a taste of dancing and modeling, I was hooked. The following summer, the Volunteer Youth Board of my town recruited people for a fashion show to raise money for the Volunteer Center. Naturally, I was first in line. The center had asked a professional fashion show organizer to run the show. There were even real models in attendance. We modeled modern clothes from the new mall in a show entitled "Autumn in Deer Park." Since this was a semiprofessional show, I knew that I had to act the part. Consequently, my cousin and I worked on some serious studly looks to provide a few laughs for my friends in the audience. I will never forget my sister's expression as she watched me unzip my skintight Gap retro sweater paired with tight black corduroy pants with trendy frayed bottoms. She was laughing so hard she couldn't even look at me. Our spirited performance helped to raise over $5,000, with half of the money going to our group, the other half to United Way. My attempt to imitate real models may have actually paid off; I received two cards from professional agencies to go to a regional model search. Tempted as I was, I found it hard to imagine giving up my Ivy League aspirations for a full-time modeling career.

However, that didn't stop me from gearing up for another Disco Fashion show junior year. I had picked up a few skills in the off-season after spending hours studying Ben Stiller as Derek Zoolander in the movie *Zoolander*. Among his other brilliant insights, he reveals the real reason why a runway is called a catwalk: "You have to be a tiger out there." At the Disco Fashion Show I armed myself with his crazy modeling moves, including a half turn of the face with shrugged shoulders and pinched lips and eyebrows, the frolic skip and turn on the runway, and the aggressive shirt throw. This year's was even more of a hit than last year's. As a result, school spirit was at its highest, and each subsequent event posted unprecedented turnouts.

Although I have all of the moves down, I would rather channel my enthusiasm for amateur modeling into working toward the goal of increasing school spirit and participation in school-wide events both in my last year of high school and in college. Keep an eye out for me— I'll be the guy at the front of the stage with polyester pants.

If this essay doesn't make you laugh, you have no sense of humor. In fact, because the rest of this student's application was so serious, this essay lightened up the tone considerably and showed his personal side. The director of admissions at a very big-name school actually took the time to handwrite a note on his acceptance letter that said something to the effect of "I hope I'll be able to pick you out on the runway." This is an excellent example of an essay that brings out a totally different facet of an applicant's personality.

This next essay is both personal and revealing.

 ## ESSAY 2

My parents filed for divorce when I was in second grade. They broke the news to me first because my sister was away. I couldn't believe it and in fact didn't believe it for the first few years even when they moved into separate houses. I suppose I was in denial, but I kept hoping they were just playing a horrible joke on us. My whole world was shattered. What I thought were immutable facts of my life had changed drastically—I no longer had two happily married parents or a stone house on Edgehill Road. I began to think the only constants in my life were my sister and our dog, who lived through the same chaos as I. My parents fought out many court battles in their custody fight, but since I was only a child, I thought they were fighting against each other, not for me. Though there are not many positive outcomes from this period of my life, I did develop a very strong bond and friendship with my sister (and dog).

Nowadays I live with my father, although I am nowhere near estranged from my mother. While I'm still close to both parents, an unsettling series of events starting at the end of my freshman year have led to the very special relationship that I have with my dad.

Three years ago, my father complained during his yearly physical of dizziness and headaches, which prompted his doctor to request a number of diagnostic tests. These revealed blockages and general plaque in an important artery found in the neck; the doctor said he needed an operation to clean the artery. The operation was short and my father was back at home before I finished school. For the next month we were flooded with get-well cards and homemade treats from neighbors and friends. All seemed well for the first six months: my father went back to playing tennis every Wednesday night and my life continued with hardly a disruption. Then suddenly his health began to deteriorate rapidly. The headaches and dizziness came back and he became progressively more lethargic. It broke my heart during soccer games when I would look from the field to see all the parents standing, cheering for their kids, while my father was sitting doubled over on the bleachers, catching his breath after the fifty-yard walk from his car. After his physical the next year, his doctor prescribed emergency open-heart, quadruple-bypass surgery. Words cannot describe how scared I was sitting at home beside my sister, waiting for hours for the doctor to call saying we could go to the hospital to see our father.

The first time I saw my father after the operation, he was lying in his hospital bed with wires protruding from different parts of his body, attached to gray machines that were keeping him alive. My father, always a strong, bold figure in my life, was incapable of completing the most rudimentary functions. Once again, I felt powerless and overwhelmed. Complications during the surgery kept my father in the hospital for two weeks while the average hospital stay for that surgery is four days. His restrictions at home were not much better than at the hospital—he was not to get out of bed for six weeks and was under constant nurse supervision for more than three months. My sister and I took on all the adult responsibilities that had formerly belonged to my dad: managing the house, paying bills, cooking and cleaning, and taking care of our father. On top of the great emotional toll, I found myself faltering at school as I let my work slide in order to spend as much time with my father as I could. Our roles were reversed as I had to make sure he was eating correctly and getting enough sleep. The hardest task was watching his diet; I had to explain to him each morning why he couldn't have his daily ration of eggs, his favorite food.

The summer before my junior year my father's health improved dramatically and I finally had some free time, which I spent backpacking in Alaska and starting a Web design business. The operation and long recovery period completely changed my relationship with my father. Now he treats me more like an adult and allows me to be more independent than most of my friends. There is an unparalleled level of trust between us. He knows that since I took care of him, I am capable of taking care of myself no matter what happens. Though it's hard to look at the bright side of such a traumatic event, I am thankful for the close bond that has developed between me and my sister and me and my father. Thanks to my independence, I feel emotionally ready to tackle the rigors of college and living on my own. I look forward to the challenges I will meet.

This essay added some very important details to the student's application. Though his grades and scores were strong, he had a weak period in tenth grade when his grades inexplicably dropped—his overall rank was very much affected by this brief drop in performance. Though he doesn't make excuses, he does explain the important information about his father's health and the additional responsibilities he assumed around the house to take care of him. In addition, the student does an excellent job of writing about his relationship with his father. He avoids the temptation to talk too much about his father. Instead, he focuses on their relationship, which helps the reader get to know him better; the essay also highlights his increased sense of responsibility and independence, skills all students need in college. In conjunction with his other essays, which were much more intellectual in nature, this essay provides the necessary personal information that could not be captured by a guidance counselor, scores, or teacher recommendations.

The next essay is one of the best I've ever read, penned by a gifted writer I'm sure we'll all be reading about in the near future.

 ESSAY 3

My best friend the first year at the Academy was a card-carrying Mozart buffoon. He could name every concerto and sonata after only a few notes and knew every Kerschel number by heart. The "Letter Duet" (*The Marriage of Figaro*) was his favorite. He was a shining Deerfield student. Bright, handsome, athletic, and rich. Archetypally rich, Gatsbyesque rich, I thought. Deerfield, like all the other boarding schools, is peopled with the scions of greatness past. Kids of politicians, actors, financiers, and kings. My friend told everybody his dad was an investment banker at Goldman Sachs. Like the rest, he wore Brooks Brothers jackets and Hermès ties to prove it.

In Charlotte, Michigan, we wore ties and jackets only at funerals and weddings. My dad owns one suit and one jacket from Penney's. Charlotte is a factory town and like everyone else there, my parents are factory workers. For most of my town that means overalls and baseball caps, a polo (style, not brand) shirt on Sundays, and perpetual battles with grease. As a kid I watched my mother scrub almost to tears to get the stuff out from beneath her fingernails before she'd go out in public at night. It also meant limited resources—for music lessons, summer camps, highfalutin vacations, and forays with things like "the arts." All I knew about Mozart, among other things, when I arrived at Deerfield was what I had read in books. In my town, listening to classical music was tantamount to requesting an ass-kicking.

Deerfield is about the furthest one can get from Charlotte. It's everything I grew up seeing in movies and books. Tall, neo-Georgian buildings rising like monsters with Ionic columns from the mists of green fields. Surrounding hills that shelter and smack of promises that invariably will be fulfilled. It's the kind of careless, rich, brilliant Eden whose mere existence gives the worry-laden Joe a strange comfort. It's why, while so different from the hot and grimy America that unfolds in every direction outside of Pockumtuck Valley, Deerfield embodies the best feelings of America. Like the vicarious hope that Paris gives to women in Nebraska, the mere existence of places such as Deerfield Academy give people like me something to ooh and aah about.

I'll never forget how shocked my parents were when a hefty admissions packet from Deerfield arrived in the mail one day my sophomore year. Was this a college? Was this a summer camp (we can't afford)? Was this a joke? My parents' voices seemed to crescendo to a shrill immediacy as I explained to them that I had requested the information . . . about (gulp) boarding schools, off a few Web sites. An are-you-crazy-we're-not-rich vaudeville followed. Mom and Dad completed each other's sentences in perfect sync. "Your dad's been laid off . . ." "and your mother's on disability!" The deeper my parents read into the material the angrier they got until I coughed out "scholarship" and a hush fell over the living room.

Deerfield came alive to me that first fall. I learned its history and its quirky traditions—like class cheers and formal dinners and letting seniors sit in the front row of the auditorium at weekly all-school meetings. I learned the school's cheering songs and its Evensong. I learned a hundred different ways to wear a sport coat. I read my first French novel (in French). I relearned proper dinner etiquette from my table head, the queenly Mrs. Matthews, and learned how to bus tables after sit-down meals (this is a rotating duty among all Deerfield students). I came to accept the way rich kids spent money and to recognize the extraordinary abilities and intellects around me.

Imagine my shock late into the year when my Mozart friend revealed to me that he was as working-class as I. He had lied. To everyone. His mother's not a Gucci-handbag mom—she's an NYC cop. His dad's not a hotshot banker—he hasn't been seen in ten years. My friend came to Deerfield three years ago on a full scholarship by way of the Boys and Girls Clubs of America. He bought the jacket and ties with the saved-up money his mother sent him each month for movies and junk food. He confessed the truth to me one night, in tears. He explained that when he came to Deerfield, everyone was so impressive and rich and so many other things that he had felt the need to fabricate something spectacular about his own life. He didn't think I'd understand that he's come to love his ability to live in the beautiful unreality he's constructed here. He didn't think I'd understand how easy it is to believe, when he looks around Deerfield, that the life he imagined up is real. But I understood. Deerfield puts you into a kind of dream state of living. It's easy to be seduced by its possibilities.

Like me, my friend had never been to an opera, though we were both fans (made possible for me by Chevron-Texaco Saturday radio broadcasts). One of the best events of my Deerfield days was going to the opera with him. We took a private car to NYC to see *La Bohème* at the Met. The whole event was ridiculously expensive, but in one of those miracles of maternal sympathy, my mother had come up with the money upon my petitioning. I think the part of her that refused to go out in public with grease under her fingernails understood why this trip was so important.

The show was amazing. Great seats, first-string cast, Zeffirelli set. We were left breathless. After dinner, we caught a cab to Penn Station and got on a train to begin our journey back to Deerfield. We bought business-class tickets. There were only a few people in our car. We bought M&Ms and soda in the café car, turned a couple of seats around, and sprawled out next to each other. We left New York at 7:00 P.M. and arrived back at Deerfield at 10:30 P.M. We watched darkness fall from the window of a train as we crept from New York, across Connecticut towns, and through southern New England. We talked about the future, college, irony, books, parents, careers, poetry, and everything.

Driving away from Deerfield Academy, from the school that has been my escape, I find myself longing to return. On bus rides home for the holidays, some part of me lingers with the picturesque campus and the arcane conversations and the long nights of work. The closer I get to Charlotte, the tawdrier the landscape gets. The signs that once announced "Historic Deerfield" now announce multiple gas-food-liquor exits, and McDonald's and Wal-Marts come into view. I think of Mozart and all I didn't know about him not very long ago, and all I don't yet know spreads out before me on the freeway and melts indistinguishably into the landscape, rising with the smoke pluming out from the factories.

Don't be intimidated—few people on the planet write this well. On top of the brilliant writing, his essay brings out crucial biographical information that begs to be heard. The subtext is, "Hey, I'm not a typical rich, spoiled prep school kid—I came from a low-income family in a factory town and made it to prep school on a scholarship." The details and rich storytelling in this essay are about as strong as you will ever see in a college essay.

This next essay is unconventional but quite charming in its originality.

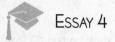 ESSAY 4

What Is Life?

Smiles. Giggles. Looking at yourself in the morning. Happiness. Your mother showing friends your naked baby pictures. Realizing you aren't what you thought you were. Having a license but no car. Falling in love. Falling out of love. Falling in love all over again. Finding a wallet on the floor and deciding what to do. Unstoppable laughter. Power. Getting buried in the sand. Fear. Never remembering what you were just talking about. Finishing a crossword all by yourself. Getting an A on a test. Getting your braces off. Never losing focus. Riding your bike for the first time. Babysitting your brother. Working hard for what you want. Learning about the birds, but never understanding the bees. Fighting over the remote control. Passion. Realizing Santa is really your father. Realizing the Easter bunny is also your father. Helping your mother bake a cake. Sticking your finger in the frosting when she isn't looking. Food fights at school. Enjoying silence. Meeting Mickey Mouse. Sitting in awe, staring at fireworks. Scoring the winning goal. Walking the dog in the rain. Asking "Would you like fries with that?" Double dipping. Dreaming of the future. Your first kiss. Losing track of time when in the deepest of conversations. Getting the phone one ring too late. Your children asking to "borrow" money. Burning your hand on that damned oven, twice. Learning how to lose. Watching all those stupid infomercials and not understanding why. Never being able to find a parking space when you need it. Watching the leaves fall in autumn; being forced to rake them up. Never "holding a kicker."* Time. The thrill of a roller coaster. Riding first class, just once. Collecting baseball cards. Denting your father's car on the mailbox. Knowledge. Fighting with a friend, then arguing over who should apologize first. A fresh cup of coffee in the morning. Getting a flat tire on the highway. Being one off of every number in the lottery. Running into old friends. Hugging your parents before you leave for college. Sinking a hole in one. Chatting on the Internet. Imagining yourself in a movie. Remembering lines from your favorite movies. Learning to say "mama." Stargazing. Sleeping in. Confusion. Thinking about nothing. Becoming a man, and realizing you can be just as immature when you want. Making fun of your best friends. Finally getting the answer to a math problem. Supergluing your hands to your desk. Irony. Telling someone what life is, in five hundred words or less.

---

*In poker, if two people have the same pair, the next highest card determines who wins. If, when drawing, a player keeps a high card (just in case this happens), it is called "holding a kicker."

This essay portrays both an extremely likable candidate, and one with lots of fresh ideas, good writing, and a dash of ingenuity to take a risk and write something funny, interesting, and even insightful in parts. After reading this essay, I had the urge to hug the author and congratulate him for not writing a boring, conventional essay. (He got into Harvard.)

Let's look at one more supplemental essay.

 ESSAY 5

John Locke once said that as children, we are born a tabula rasa, a blank slate, and that our immediate surroundings create how we view the world.

Since kindergarten, I have attended the oldest Waldorf school in America. Waldorf education, created by the Austrian philosopher Rudolf Steiner, reflects Locke's belief that students must create their own perceptions of the world and not allow their surroundings to shape who they become. Growing up with this education, even while living in New York City, I was allowed to absorb only "the purest, most beneficial information" that would enable me to develop into a whole, balanced being.

In kindergarten, instead of learning my ABCs and multiplication tables, I was given blank sheets of recycled, natural paper and an array of waxy, block crayons and told to express myself. Faceless dolls were put in front of me, in lieu of Barbies, so that I could imagine and create my own experience of what the dolls' facial expressions looked like. I learned to knit, to shape animals with natural beeswax, and to explore the wonders of nature and of my imagination in Sheep's Meadow, Central Park. I never consumed soda or sweets. I never ingested Western medicine. I never used Crayola crayons. I never watched television.

As I got older, I left this sheltered life for the inevitable: reality. Living in such a diverse, heterogeneous place as New York City, I slowly began to see the world from the perspectives of those who had not grown up within an Austrian philosopher's educational cocoon. Of all the differences I perceived between my Waldorf world and that of the "outside," the biggest dilemma I found was the way in which television and film—something that I was just barely beginning to become familiar with in my 'tween years—influence society.

As I got older, I would go over to my friend's house and curiously consent to watch television for the morning. I'd watch as she flipped through channels. But what I found even more fascinating than the shows we viewed was the way in which she became hypnotized, almost, by the television. She wouldn't respond when I asked her a question. I would poke her until she at least gave me a grunt or a slight nod.

I wondered why, if television had such a powerful impact on people, it couldn't be used to uplift or teach. I saw the disparities between myself and my friend, who grew up watching *Barney* and *Sesame Street,* and came home after school every evening to view her daily dose of *Will and Grace.* Television and film shaped who she was, it seemed . . . it had filled her tabula rasa with the producer's choices, not her own.

I had a passionate desire to be the person controlling the images on that screen, the master puppeteer who had the power to influence my friend's thoughts and actions. But instead of displaying content that just dulled and made her passive, I wanted her to become motivated and inspired to action.

Interning at the New York headquarters of Globo TV, Brazil's largest television network, two summers ago, I experienced this impact of merging social issues and entertainment to create social change. Globo has been a pioneer in this field; its most popular form of television, *novelas,* combine stories with controversial social issues. By drawing its audience into issues through compelling stories, Globo's *novelas* were able to change the public's opinions in a profound and sweeping manner, transforming views on prejudice and gender issues.

My work at Globo TV led me to enroll in the Oxford Tradition at Oxford University this summer. Amongst the glorious towers and magnificent old buildings of Oxford University, I sat between the looming bookshelves of the Bodleian Library, discussing with my professor the effects of the media and how we can change it. During lighter moments, Professor A. talked to us about the power we have to awaken our audience and "capture the magic." For the first time, I felt the power of cradling the video camera in my hands and looking through the lens into a different world. I felt the power of manipulating what I saw in reality and transforming it into something entirely different for the viewer.

My studies at Oxford confirmed for me, from a historical, theoretical, and hands-on perspective, the power of the media and its potential to create positive social change. From my unique upbringing in Waldorf education, my tabula rasa is filled with a passionate desire to impact society so people don't evolve to reflect the negative influences of their surroundings, but are instead brought up to become whole, balanced human beings who are motivated to contribute to the transformation of a more harmonious world community. Stay tuned.

While this student's main essay focused on her academic interests, she felt that the essence of who she really was didn't come across. So in her extra essay she focused on her unusual background, what makes her unique, and how she became interested in film and media. Clearly she comes across as the type of student who would add diversity and her own unique persona to the class. She makes the reader *want* to stay tuned.

Learning Differences

For students who have serious learning disabilities, it is advisable to use the supplemental essay to write a short learning statement. This allows students a forum to express the nature of the disability, how they have compensated for it, and how it affects their learning. Colleges will not use this information against a student so long as there is no evidence in the transcript, the teacher recommendations, or the written material of major academic struggles. In other words, unless the college is concerned that you will not be able to handle the level of academic rigor (and that concern cannot come only from your essay—they are not allowed to discriminate), there is no reason not to take the time to explain your learning differences. The most appropriate title is "Statement of Learning Differences." Let's read an actual example from a student who was accepted to all of his top-choice colleges.

 ESSAY 6

My thirst for knowledge has enabled me to overcome some mild learning differences, so much so that I am a consistent honor roll student and a member of the honor society. Ironically, the subject that is the hardest for me is also one of the ones I enjoy most. I've always enjoyed literature (some of my favorites are *The Great Gatsby, The Crucible, A Rose for Emily . . .*), but I have to go through a totally different process than most students in order to understand and appreciate what I am reading. First I try to get as much as I can out of the story from a first slow read-through. Then I'll read some parts out loud, and finally I'll read through it again until I've been able to synthesize what I've covered. I think in some ways this process has allowed me to reach a deeper understanding of what I read, since I end up spending so much time poring over the text.

My learning differences have also taught me to be an advocate for myself. I utilize all the extra help that is available to me during school hours and after school and I go the extra mile to seek additional help when needed. If I know I'm struggling to understand a particular subject, I'll work with a tutor until I feel completely comfortable with the material. If I need extra time for a test, I discuss my needs directly with my teachers. I don't like to make excuses for my learning differences—that's why I feel so strongly about being my own advocate. Thanks to my strong preparation, I always end up doing very well on tests and quizzes. In high school, I've become completely independent both on the academic front and on the personal front. Since my mom is a single parent who works long hours, I help her out by driving myself to and from school, making my own meals, doing my own laundry, and helping to maintain the house.

Just as I manage my studies, I have learned to be an inventive planner. When my family decided to plan a trip last summer, they turned to me to organize all the details from airfare, hotels, and car rentals to sightseeing. (And they don't even give me a percentage!) I use a variety of Internet travel sites to compare prices, negotiate rates, and pick the best routes for all our family trips. All my friends turn to me when they need hard-to-find tickets for sporting events because they know I am tenacious and creative enough to locate them. When my Internet searches come up blank, I've been known to call obscure parts of the state to find local tickets that are not available nationwide. I even got ahold of the elusive Marlins-Indians World Series tickets for my family. My crowning achievement involved laying my hands on the impossible-to-find playoff tickets of archrivals Miami Heat and New York Knicks. Although most people would view having a learning disability as a negative trait, I've been able to use it to my advantage by becoming my own advocate and by reaching a higher level of independence.

With a nice dose of humor, this student not only details the nature of his disability but also emphasizes the specific methods he uses to overcome his problems. Colleges want to make sure that their students know how to advocate for themselves and that they understand the nature of their problem. Most ·colleges have learning centers, but students need to take the initiative to seek out these services. This student would obviously seek help immediately if he were to fall behind. Therefore, no college was concerned that he might have serious academic problems.

In summary, the purpose of the supplemental essay is to illuminate some part of your persona that would not otherwise be clear from the rest of the application. It also provides you with a chance to explain any major problems or factors that may have influenced your academic performance or explain a learning difficulty. Though you don't want to dwell too much on your problems, you do want to at least allude to them so that an admissions committee can hear your explanation. This is the time to write your most personal essay on something that has meant a lot to you. Though it is not required, it should be clear after reading the examples in this chapter that this one essay can add an entirely different dimension to your application. Take advantage of this opportunity.

6
ODDBALL ESSAYS

While the trend has been toward accepting the Common Application and adding a short supplemental essay question supplied by the particular school (simply point your browser to www.commonapp.org and you can see a table of every school that takes the Common Application, plus a link to their supplemental forms), some schools stubbornly refuse to bend to the will of the Common Application. The most notorious of these (I mean this in a good way, as I enjoy their application) are MIT and the University of Chicago. The University of Chicago goes so far as to actually label its application "The unCommon Application" to highlight that it is proud of its individuality. Even though MIT goes out of its way to create a unique application, there's nothing on the application that should throw anyone who has been reading

Acing the College Application up to this point. First are some short-answer questions: "We know you lead a busy life, full of activities, many of which are required of you. Tell us about something you do simply for the pleasure of it. (This isn't a trick question. We want to see how you bring balance to your life.)" Knowing the type of student who typically attends MIT, it's probably a good idea for the college to make sure there *is* something just for fun that each student does. It obviously is trying to combat its reputation as a rigorous school that is known as an academic pressure cooker. I've had students answer this question with a great deal of light-hearted fun, talking about fantasy football addictions, baseball card collecting, stargazing, hiking, watching *Desperate Housewives*, the whole gamut. With this kind of question you should make your answer short and let your individuality shine through. If you spend your free time knitting, say so!

There's nothing that crazy about MIT's short-answer questions. As for its main essay, you have a choice of two:

Essay A: Tell us about an experience which, at the time, really felt like "the end of the world"—but had it not happened, you would not be who you are today. Describe the process through which you discovered value in the negative.

Essay B: Describe the world you come from, for example, your family, clubs, school, community, city or

town. How has that world shaped your dreams and as-
pirations?

The second essay is the more "personal" one, equivalent
to the supplemental essay. In many cases, my students actually just use the supplemental essay they already wrote and
simply add a few lines to adapt it to fit Essay B. Essay A
would require a separate response if you had something
gripping in mind. My advice would be to opt for Essay A if
there is an event that had a major impact on you (the earlier
main essay we saw about the boy whose father was killed in
the World Trade Center attack would fit perfectly for this
one), but barring that, I'd suggest Essay B, which would give
any student a chance to talk more about him- or herself on a
personal level and add another dimension to the application.

In short, the MIT application is more conventional than
you might think.

In my opinion, the school that deserves the "uncommon"
moniker is the University of Chicago. It is proud of the fact
that admitted students design their essay questions every
year—it even announces the process right on the application: "To develop this year's extended essay options, we
e-mailed the students who had been admitted last year and
asked them for topics. We received several hundred responses, many of which were eloquent, intriguing, or down-
right wacky. As you can see by the attributions, the questions
below were inspired by submissions from your peers."

Before you arrive at the main essays, the University of Chicago application does have two short-response essays, but these again are very straightforward. The first asks basically why you are interested in the University of Chicago in the first place (as we'll see in the next chapter, that is the "why" paragraph), and the second is reminiscent of the MIT short question: "Please tell us about a few of your favorite books, poems, authors, films, pieces of music," and so on. The goal here is to have some fun, express your individuality, and show that you are not just a total geek.

No school has a more original main essay than the University of Chicago, although they may bow to the pressure to accept the Common Application and eliminate their unique questions. You have two major options. If you're pressed for time, choose Option 5, the last question, which is basically totally open-ended. You can use your main essay from the Common Application and simply make your own prompt that fits your response. I have several students who do that. But because the University of Chicago seeks out students up to the challenge of responding to one of the more esoteric questions, I'd highly recommend writing an outrageous essay. One of my most brilliant math/economics students wrote one of the best essays I've ever read, which I think tells Chicago, "Hey, I enjoyed your crazy essay topic and I've taken it and torn it up for your reading pleasure!" Let's take a look.

Essay Option 4

The Cartesian coordinate system is a popular method of representing real numbers and is the bane of eighth graders everywhere. Since its introduction by Descartes in 1637, this means of visually characterizing mathematical values has swept the globe, earning a significant role in branches of mathematics such as algebra, geometry, and calculus. Describe yourself as a point or series of points on this axial arrangement. If you are a function, what are you? In which quadrants do you lie? Are x and y enough for you, or do you warrant some love from the z-axis? Be sure to include your domain, range, derivative, and asymptotes, should any apply. Your possibilities are positively and negatively unbounded.

As a budding mathematician, I could not resist writing about the Cartesian coordinate system. (I have even been accused of calling calculus "nature's poetry.") When I actually sat down and thought about Mr. Nalven's question, however, I quickly realized that the question does not make strict mathematical (or logical) sense. A function is defined as "the relationship or correspondence between two or more variables." Similarly, the Cartesian coordinate system consists of at least two axes. So to describe myself as a point or a series of points on this axial arrangement is not enough— I need to involve at least one more variable, as I only count as one variable.

So I needed a control group. I guess it makes sense—after all, you can't simply say that "the University of Chicago is better," you have to say that "the University of Chicago is better than any other university in the world" to be grammatically correct and to be meaningful. (The University of Chicago really is better than any other university in the world; it turns out that a study done at the U of C was responsible for taxis being yellow. I don't see any other university determining the color of taxicabs!) Since this is an application essay to the U of C, I think that it is completely appropriate for me to compare myself to the U of C.

To achieve that goal, I emulated Samuelson; I "mathematicized" my life (just like Samuelson brought mathematics into economics) by assigning numerical values to several aspects of my life (for example, 64.06, the country and area code of Wanganui [New Zealand]) and pairing them with corresponding numerical values of the U of C. Then I plotted them on the Cartesian coordinate system so I could investigate whether there was any relationship between those points, and voilà—a very simple trend curve with R^2 value of 0.993 was formed. Essentially, this means that there is such a strong relationship between the numerical values assigned to the U of C and the ones assigned to me that a very simple model that matches with the original data 99 percent of the time could be formed. I went through the exact same process with Harvard—I used all my data analysis techniques, but the model with the highest R^2 only had an R^2 value of 0.34. Apparently Harvard and I are like water and oil and the U of C and I are like hydrogen and oxygen atoms— you could say that if the University of Chicago were a person, he would be my twin.

The Comparison Between Me and the U of C

$$y = -6E-10x^4 + 3E-06x^3 - 0.0048x^2 + 2.9504x - 5.4866$$
$$R^2 = 0.993$$

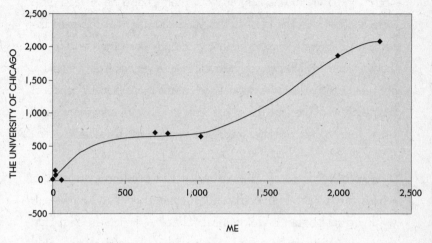

This is what my function looks like on the Cartesian coordinate system. The function is positively and negatively unbounded—unlimited domain and range. It is worth noting the derivative of this function: $\frac{-3x^4}{1250000000} + \frac{9x^2}{1000000} - .0096x + 2.9504$. For example, $(4,8)$ (the number of math awards I won, the number of the National Medal of Science associated with the U of C) has a positive slope of 2.91—looks like both I and the U of C mathematicians are in line for a *lot* more awards. We share many attributes, including ages—both the U of C and I are relatively younger than our peers (and trust me, being the only twelve-year-old in a PE class with fourteen- and fifteen-year-olds is not fun. Oh yeah, did I mention that I am flat-footed?). We may be young, but we are as smart as our more experienced peers. It is just that we will never get to play for the Chicago White Sox.

In conclusion, the mathematical analysis of me and the University of Chicago provides irrefutable evidence that I belong in the university. According to my rudimentary analysis, there should be at least 500 more applicants to the U of C this year; knowing that this particular person is definitely admitted ought to slightly ease the pressure and the workload. My interviewer, Gabrielle, was a very nice person (plus, I got free fruit thanks to her suggestion to visit the Graduate School of Business), and I presume that she is representative of admissions counselors. I am happy that I have made your work a little bit easier!

You have to admit that even for the academic superstars who apply to the University of Chicago, this essay sparkles. If we lived in England, we'd call it "cheeky." I like the fact that the student insults Harvard and "proves" mathematically that he's a much better match for Chicago than he is for Harvard. The admissions office would have loved that part, as they consider themselves at least Harvard's equal. Note how the writer mixes his two areas of strength, math modeling and economics, and *shows* us his strengths by coming up with a graph to represent his personality and how it fits with the University of Chicago. He took what looked like an impossible question and knocked that baseball right out of the park. It's an essay worthy of such an arcane question.

The lesson? If you enjoy this kind of exercise, you would probably feel right at home at the University of Chicago. If it's torture for you, you may want to think twice about applying to a school that prides itself on nearly impossible application questions.

7

THE "WHY" PARAGRAPH

Despite their oddball application essays, both MIT and the University of Chicago made sure to ask *why* you were interested in applying to these schools in the first place. Some other non–Common Application schools or those that have special supplemental questions also take the time to ask why you think you are a good match for their school (the University of Pennsylvania, for example, goes out of its way to ask why you are interested in Penn).

But the important part for us is that 99 percent of the colleges out there do *not* ask why you are applying to them in the first place. That's one problem I have with the Common Application. Colleges are falling over themselves to accept the Common Application so it looks like they are welcoming to minorities and lower-income kids (who can simply fill out one application and photocopy it for as many schools as they apply to), but in the process of democratizing their application, they lost the particular flavor of what makes their school special. The moral of the story? Colleges *want* to know (1) that you love their school, and for the right reasons (not just that it's a pretty campus, but because you love their academic programs) and (2) that you are a good match. After all, if you want to study Sanskrit and you apply to some small college in Kansas, the odds are it will not have a big department of Indo-European languages. What this means for the student is that you should take the time for every school on your list to write a school-specific "why" paragraph that focuses on why you are a good match, what attracts you to the school, what programs stand out, and why you are dying to go. Yes, even for schools that don't take the time to add a "why" paragraph to their supplemental forms, you should simply put a header on the top of the page, write "Why I Want to Go to X College" on top, and write a paragraph or two about why you want to attend.

Because the University of Chicago actually takes the time to ask why you are applying, let's look at the "why" paragraph from the same student who wrote the Cartesian coordinate essay.

The word "university" is from the Latin word "universitas," which means "society, guild." Universities used to be the forums for erudite men to discuss ideas. Unfortunately most universities today have become the places for vocational training, not for scholarly study.

Money only represents the relative satisfaction, utility, and is only a mere tool that allows us to compare apples to oranges. Many times I wonder why we are so fixated about money—I mean, we are not nearly as crazy about other measuring tools!

Holden Caulfield in *The Catcher in the Rye* said that "certain things should stay the way they are. You ought to be able to stick them in one of those big glass cases and just leave them alone. I know that's impossible, but it's too bad anyway." Personally, I believe the University of Chicago is one of those "certain things." The university's insistence on Common Core, its lack of vocational majors, and The unCommon Application itself ensure that the U of C remains true to the real meaning of "university." I have visited many great universities, yet the only university I can see myself attending is the University of Chicago. The prospectus of the *real* university with its students and professors "seeking the higher truth" is simply irresistible. (I am cynical and disdainful about all vocational majors and professional schools except the U of C's Graduate School of Business—it gives out free fruit!)

I also have a penchant for the rigorousness of the courses at the university; I personally believe that repetition and hardship is the one and only way to make oneself better. The Spartan army was the strongest in ancient Greece—ask any Persian who was at Thermopylae, he would vouch for me—because its solders were trained from the age of seven. I am not a person who backs down from challenge, and I am not going to cower away from "where fun comes to die" and "where the only thing that goes down is your GPA." I know that I will walk out of the U of C with four years of world-class education, and I do not care that I will probably have to pull one too many all-nighters to keep up. Sleeping is overrated! Sure, the research shows that people my age should sleep between 10:00 P.M. and 4:00 A.M. because growth hormones are created at that time, but hey, I am already 5'11", so I'm not worried.

Finally, the reputation of the U of C's economics department is legendary. The University of Chicago also has top mathematics and statistics departments, which are essential to any economics education. Of course there are other top economics departments, but in the field of economics that I am particularly interested in, economic development, the U of C has two of the best professors in the field—Professors Fogel and Lucas. The economics department also has Steven Levitt! I read many of his papers before I purchased his popular book *Freakonomics,* and my marginal utility (satisfaction) from the book was not that great since I already knew "why drug dealers lived with their mothers." I demanded a refund of income he earned from my purchasing of the book, but Professor Levitt declined to respond to my e-mail. He only left me with the option of getting into the U of C and suffering through four sleepless years of world-class education just so that I can meet him in person and get my dollar back. (Rest assured that I will be keeping track of inflation to make sure that Professor Levitt pays me in real terms. A buck now would probably have half that purchasing power in 2007.)

Clearly this student has done his research! He knows all about the university in a way that shows he spent a significant amount of time researching the specifics of the departments he was interested in, the professors who taught there, and the course material. As it turned out, in his field of math modeling and economics, Chicago and Dartmouth College had the strongest programs. This brings up a point worth mentioning—the very process of researching the information you need in your "why" paragraph will actually lead you to figure out which schools really are a good match for you! Colleges will not be impressed if you apply just because of the name recognition factor of the school. That would be the worst possible reason. And deep down, you shouldn't be applying to a college based on name alone. That would be like wearing Seven Jeans just for the brand name even though they make you look like a fat blimp. Like the jeans, college must be a good fit. You want to make sure you are applying to a college for the right reason. If you are looking for small classes, no TAs, and individualized attention from professors, you would be more suited to small liberal arts colleges such as Amherst, Middlebury, and Williams than you would be to larger schools such as Harvard, the University of Chicago, and Stanford.

One easy way to use an existing essay as the basis of your "why" paragraph is to take the extra essay you already wrote on your most meaningful intellectual experience and add one or two paragraphs to it. That way you'll have more substance to your essay. Be sure also to mention any visits to the campus, contact with professors, class observations (I highly recommend that you try to attend a class when you visit a campus), et cetera to show that you've done due diligence about finding the fit.

Let's look at two other examples of "why" paragraphs:

As the tires of my car roll over the heavily salted highway, I let my mind wonder about the chemical properties of salt, the centripetal force that enables my car to round corners, and how to calculate my stopping distance using energy equations from physics. Passing through the autumn landscape above X's Second Beach while I am running cross-country, I speculate about why our coastal course always seems windier, or what has caused me to reach my anaerobic threshold, or how to use Newton's third law to confirm that friction is the sole force propelling me forward, while I should be focusing on running. My biology teacher aptly called such ruminations the "curse of the scientist." If I'm not talking or really focusing on something, I'm thinking, most likely about science.

"Scio, scire, scivi, scitum," the Latin verb meaning "to know," and its English derivative, "science," exemplify my quest for knowledge, especially in the field of science. From biology to chemistry to physics to my summer classes in human physiology and biotechnology, I've immersed myself in as much science as possible. I hope to continue this quest at the University of Pennsylvania with the chance to study with top-notch professors and researchers. Although I presently wish to major in chemistry, Penn's biochemistry and biophysics courses also attract me with their combination of science disciplines. When I visited Penn, I was especially impressed by the science labs and research facilities and could see myself continuing my research there.

Along with science, I also wish to continue my study of Latin. Penn's Classical Studies Department offers advanced courses in the Latin language in conjunction with the history and the literature of the classical period. The courses on Cicero's *Letters,* Roman satire, Latin historical documents, and Greek will offer me the advanced level of study I am seeking after AP Latin V. In addition, having been frustrated as a child by the Latin inscriptions that I could not decipher on the Roman monuments, I also would relish the opportunity to return to Italy both speaking Italian and reading Latin at a high level. Penn would provide this opportunity, maybe even with an archeological focus.

Penn fits my interests outside the classroom as well. Penn's urban location provides meaningful community service opportunities. In Philadelphia, I can continue my work with, and promotion of, Big Brothers and explore other community service areas as well. The extracurricular clubs and intramural sports at Penn also offer community involvement and leadership opportunities that I found so important in high school. On campus, the college house system serves as a great way to meet and share mutual interests with classmates from all over the world.

From every vantage point, right down to its location across from Fresh Grocer, Penn is the school where I would fit in best and contribute to both inside and outside the classroom. Having played scores of tennis tournaments wearing a Penn hat from my brother, I don't have to stretch my imagination much to see myself wearing my own hat.

This student shows through his detailed example that he knows his main interests (science and classics) and he knows that Penn is strong in these two areas. Because his brother attended Penn, he mentions the family connections (if you're a legacy, feel free to describe your parent's influence on your interest in the school). Note how his first paragraphs are general enough to use for more than one college, so he has only to add the school-specific part at the end—that saved him a good deal of time.

Here's another example of how a student took his essay on his most meaningful intellectual experience and tacked on the "why" paragraph:

Cameras were rolling as I stepped onto the homemade platform sporting red tights and a velvet, harlequin sleeved tunic. My words imitated Old English as I announced the upcoming jousting tournament between Sir William Marshal, the Earl of Pembroke, and AJ the Pitiful. This scene was one of many I directed for my ninth-grade history class project. Our job was to create a two-minute videotaped commercial selling some aspect of life in medieval times. After extensive research using primary and secondary sources on medieval life and advertising tips found in *Ogilvy on Advertising,* I developed the idea of selling padded armor typically worn under chain mail. I chose to promote padded armor (I took the liberty of calling it underwear) in order to give our advertisement an element of humor, surprise, and creativity. I felt that rather than using the path of predictability I would have encountered had I chosen to advertise jousting, lances, or catapults (all of which I explored), an unexpected twist would be both more attention-getting and memorable. Sir William Marshal, famed as the champion of five hundred tournaments during his time period (c. 1150s–1219), represented my endorsement representative. I designed a storyboard for the product, called "Knights' Knickers." It was customary for the loser of the joust to relinquish his chain mail to his opponent; therefore the slogan was "Keep your pride when you've lost your lance and your pants. Buy Knight's Knickers: finest underpants." The commercial won "best commercial" because of its creativity, authenticity, documented research, and effectiveness. What I enjoyed the most about this project was incorporating the different disciplines (history, film, music, and advertising) to learn about a particular time period. I used this interdisciplinary approach in my English class. Some of my works on film have been various scenes from Kurt Vonnegut's *Slaughterhouse-Five,* Fitzgerald's *The Great Gatsby,* Homer's *Odyssey,* and Michael Crichton's *Jurassic Park.*

Although I can envision myself taking part in the film club at college, I am drawn to Haverford's interdisciplinary approach in their science programs as well. While visiting your campus, I was able to tour the Marian E. Koshland Integrated Natural Sciences Center. I was impressed with the facility and the idea that I could be doing undergraduate research in the "superlab" as early as my junior year. Haverford College represents the best of both worlds in that the tri-college system makes it feel like a university with the personal attention of a small college setting. I'm applying early because it is by far my first-choice college and I know I will receive a strong liberal arts education while still pursuing my passion for music both in class (Jazz and the Politics of Culture) and outside of the classroom in the Haverford funk band, Hiram.

As you might guess, small colleges especially want to see that their college is at the top of your list, not that you're just applying as an Ivy League reject. In fact, that's why it's super important to take the time to write a "why" paragraph even when the school doesn't ask. With the recent trend of abolishing early decision or early action programs at some schools (including Princeton, Harvard, the University of Virginia, and the University of Delaware), it's even more important to indicate if a college is your top choice and why. In the past, the very fact of applying early decision meant the college was your clear first choice, but as more schools rely solely on regular decision, the more important it will be to emphasize that you have done your research and that you indeed are interested in a school.

Why do colleges care? In a word, "yield." It looks much better when a high percentage of students who are offered a place in the freshman class accept the offer of admission. Colleges such as Harvard pride themselves on high yield rates, and admissions directors are often graded, in part, on how good a job they do convincing students to accept their offer over that of another school. All the top colleges track who they "lose" students to, so they are more likely to accept a student who shows an undying devotion to their school and who takes the time to show that their school is at the top of his or her list. In short, this is the reason the "why" paragraph is so important. No matter what else you do, take the time to do your research and write a well-thought-out paragraph that explains in some detail why you are a good fit for each college and why you want to attend. For close cases, this will be the essay that makes or breaks your application.

8

A STEP-BY-STEP LOOK AT THE DATA SECTION OF THE APPLICATION

Luckily for Common Application users, you'll have to fill out the four data pages of the application only one time because you can then photocopy them and use the copies for any college that accepts the Common Application. I recommend handwriting or typing the Common Application forms for each application rather than simply photocopying them. Though much of this section is self-explanatory (name, address), there are some important points that students often ask about. Let's take it page by page.

 ## PAGE 1 OF THE COMMON APPLICATION

The first few lines with name and address really are obvious until you get down to *mailing address for admissions correspon-*

dence. This is mostly for students who attend boarding schools. What you write really depends on where you will be when decision letters are mailed. For early decision, the letters arrive between December 8 and 16, and for regular decision they come in early April. If you want to be sure to have the letter sent to your home, leave it blank (which means they'll send it to the official mailing address), but if you'll still be at your school and want to receive it there, write down your school address, making sure to include your individual box number.

Citizenship. They ask about your citizenship because of financial aid concerns, but also so they can determine how to classify you in the admissions pool. Technically, if you are a dual citizen you could be considered an international student, but for the most part, it's much better to be an American citizen for admissions purposes or a U.S. student living abroad. Because you have to tell the truth, it really is a moot point—if you're a U.S. citizen check off that box.

Possible areas of academic concentration/major. Colleges really shouldn't be asking you this because a common major such as politics or English will only work against you. On the other hand, if you say you are interested in some obscure subject (such as entomology, as long as the college has that department), it could help you. Colleges are not supposed to use this information in making an admissions decision because these answers rarely correspond with what a student actually majors in, but they often do because it's there. My advice is that if you are thinking of putting down economics, government, or some other very common major, just check off "undecided." However, if you do have a more atypical interest, write it in. My feeling is that it's none of their business—how can a high school senior really know what he may major in? I changed majors four times in college, and most of my friends followed suit. Not to mention that lots of students start in the premed track, but many fewer follow it all the way through.

Possible career or professional plans. If it's a liberal arts school and you want to be an investment banker, say you're "undecided."

Will you be a candidate for financial aid? If the school is 100 percent need-blind and you think you will qualify for aid, by all means check off "yes." If you can get by without aid and the school is *not* need-blind, you're better off not applying for it. Remember, the most elite colleges are actively recruiting low-income students, so at the Ivies and top liberal arts colleges, it will *help* you to check off "yes."

Optional—Place of birth. This one is a mystery to me. I have no idea why they want to know unless it's in case you were born in some exotic locale and speak another language (see following).

Social Security number. Write it in if you have one.

First language if other than English, language spoken at home. These questions will only help you, so if you were born speaking Swedish and still speak it, by all means include the information. This information is also used to explain the SAT verbal scores—a student whose first language is Russian may understandably have a lower verbal score, so admissions officers need to know about the other language. If you learned English only recently and have a very low verbal score, the college may ask you to take the TOEFL (Test of English as a Foreign Language) exam.

Optional—Ethnic information. Students always ask me if they should leave this whole section blank. Because it's optional, you can do that. Unless you fall into one of the recruited minority groups (black, Hispanic, or Native American), the information will not help you and could actually hurt you (in the case of a surfeit of Asian applicants). On the other hand, if you are mixed-race and at least half black or Hispanic, you should identify with the less common group, as it will put you in the minority category for recruiting purposes (so if you're half white and half African American, for example, I'd suggest you check off the latter). If you are mixed race but not 50 percent of any one race, then you need to check "other" and list the individual races.

 ## PAGE 2 OF THE COMMON APPLICATION

Educational data. It does seem somewhat superfluous to fill out all the school information, because your guidance counselor will include a transcript and a profile, but you have to fill it out completely so that the admissions staff will know about where you go to school before they arrive at the counselor material. They usually read your part of the application first and then the counselor's part and the teacher recommendations. For *date of graduation,* you can put just the month—no one cares about the exact date. They are only asking to see if you are on track to graduate in the spring of your senior year. Under *other secondary schools, including summer schools and programs,* you want to list not only other high schools you may have attended, but also any academic summer programs. Remember, the admissions committee is looking for initiative in seeking out challenges, so it is often helpful to have attended either some summer programs or other classes that show you have pursued your studies outside the bounds of your high school. Notice that the very next item is *list all colleges at which you have taken courses for credit.* Here is where you list the actual courses you took at an official college or community college in your area. You should list the course even if it was not for a grade—just write "credit, no grade" to show that it was not graded. Right underneath are two short questions—one is not applicable to the majority of applicants, but if you have a GED rather than a high school diploma, list the date you received it. The next question asks for detail if your education was interrupted for any reason, so if that is relevant, add an explanation.

Test information. Two key points for this section: Be sure to list not only all the tests you have taken and want to report, but also the names and dates of any tests you are planning to take. Often admissions officers will look at this section and say, "Boy, this first SAT I really was low—but at least I can see that Joe is signed up to take it again so we can see how he does." What you don't want is to look like you're sitting pretty on your mediocre scores and not doing anything to improve them.

The second key point is that you'll notice there is no space here for either Advanced Placement (AP) scores or International Baccalaureate (IB) scores. That might give you the impression that these scores don't count, but that is not the case. In fact, because both AP and IB tests are considered the most difficult and college-like tests around, colleges sometimes weigh these even more heavily than the SAT I and SAT II. These tests are more oriented toward essays and deep thinking compared to the relatively straightforward multiple choice tests of the SATs. Moreover, a strong showing on these tests (most students have either AP or IB at their high schools, although a few high schools offer both programs) can counterbalance some less than stellar scores elsewhere. Therefore a student who scores only a 650 verbal on the SAT I but gets a 5 on the AP literature exam shows a much stronger reading ability than the verbal score alone would indicate. Rather than have you write your AP/IB scores in this section, the new Common Application asks you to include them in the academic honors section on page 3, so be patient.

Page 3 of the Common Application

Family. I would group these family questions under the none-of-your-damned-business category. Therefore, I would offer as little information as possible. The only key piece of data that admissions officers should legitimately use is where your parents went to college, and the *only* reason they should know this is to establish whether you will be considered a legacy at that particular school. If your mom graduated from Yale, you would be considered a legacy, a designation that would roughly double your chance of admission. Note that the status is generally awarded only for undergraduate colleges. (There are some exceptions, most notably the University of Pennsylvania, so it's always worth checking directly with the school.) In other words, just because your father or mother attended Harvard Law School or Harvard Business School does not make you a legacy at Harvard College.

If the legacy factor is the only legitimate fact in the family section, why do colleges want to know more information? Let's look at the best- and worst-case scenarios. Best case: Neither of your parents attended college at all, your father is a factory worker, and your mom is on disability. Colleges will see that you are definitely from a lower socioeconomic and nonprivileged background, so your achievements will be read against that profile. In this case, the information will help your candidacy. All the elite colleges make a tremendous effort to recruit low-income and non-college-background students, so by all means take advantage of this fact. Worst case: Your father went to Yale as an undergraduate and then to Harvard Business School and is now an investment banker, and your mom went to Brown, holds a Ph.D. in chemistry, and works as a research chemist. Common sense dictates that colleges should want to attract students like you from successful, well-educated parents, and most students I've worked with have believed this. But in the age of diversity and multiculturalism, this kind of upbringing will only work against you. Suddenly, you'll find admissions officers asking questions like this: "Obviously, his family can afford SAT prep—why aren't his scores higher?" "How come this student has never held a job?" "Why isn't she getting all A's in chemistry—I mean, her mom should be able to help her out, right?" "He doesn't look like he's sought out challenges—everything has been handed to him on a silver platter."

Of course, some of these questions can be legitimate, but as you can see, most of them border on the impertinent. Many assumptions will be made based on your address, your high school, and what your parents do for a living. My recommendation is to force admissions officers to look at you as a student first, not as a scion of a wealthy family. You can do this by providing as little information as possible. You can't lie about where they attended school, but you can be vague when it comes to addressing *name of business or organization* and *occupation*. Rather than putting down "Goldman Sachs" and "investment banker," volunteer only "finance" and "banking." If your mom is the chief neurosurgeon for a New York hospital, try "medical" for occupation or just "doctor." Is this lying? I don't think it is as long as you don't lie! If the information will only hurt you, why should you volunteer it? After all, do you want to be judged by what your parents do or by what your own achievements are? All students should be judged on their own merit.

Siblings. This just gives the admission committee some idea of how many kids are in your family and what kind of schools they attend. You really can't manipulate this one at all, so just list them. Although siblings don't give legacy status officially, colleges will certainly give you a closer look if others in your family have attended their college.

Extracurricular, personal, and volunteer activities. For any application except the Common Application, you can simply write, "Please see attached activity list" and enclose the list we spoke of earlier. However, one annoying feature of the Common Application is that it specifically says to highlight your activities in the space it provides even if you plan on attaching an additional sheet. So take out your trusty pen and neatly write in your seven most important activities. This should be very easy for those who have already completed the full activity list. If you think there is a chance of your participating in this activity in college, by all means check off that box. In addition, in the space right over the chart itself, write in big letters "Please see attached activity list" to remind the admissions committee that you have prepared a more complete list.

Academic honors. Here's the general rule: If you have only one or two academic honors, just write them in, but if you have many, you should type them up in an organized list. In the latter instance, simply write, "Please see attached award list." Unfortunately, the directions do not remind you again to self-report your AP or IB scores, so I'll remind you: List them here! The instructions are actually back under the directions for the test information section of the Common Application.

 PAGE 4 OF THE COMMON APPLICATION

Work experience. Leave this section blank at your own peril, and be forewarned that babysitting and camp counseling are considered cushy jobs (even though those of us who have done them know that is not the case). You can also list your own business here if you have started a small one such as tutoring, computer design, or anything else you do. Again, you don't need to write it on this page as long you have included a separate section on your activity list for work experience. Simply write, "Please see attached activity list for work experience." Be sure to include summer employment, too, because it specifically asks about it.

Short answer. This asks you to briefly elaborate on one of your activities. See, I told you the essay you wrote on this would come in handy.

Personal essay. This last section is the personal statement.

Because you will have already written it, all you need to do is check off which question you have answered. If you've written a personal essay, as I have suggested, you may want to belatedly invent your question (option number six—topic of your choice) and write in the space below. If you wrote an essay about your obsessive devotion to computer languages and how you got started, try a question such as "Describe a childhood hobby that you never let go." Try to make the question a tad more zippy than a generic "Tell us about something that interests you."

You'll notice that in the essay chapter I didn't break down the Common Application essays into the six choices. That's because I think it's important to work backward from what you want to write about to the question. Think about it philosophically for a moment. Most students simply go through the application step by step and respond to each question as they happen upon it. That is why most students write boring applications—they are trying to fit their interesting lives into boring questions. I've found that students write much more lively and personal essays if they think long and hard about what they want to write first and then worry about the question. Colleges are less concerned with finding the answer to a specific question than they are in getting to know you. Often they won't even remember what question they asked as long you provide an interesting and thoughtful answer. If you follow my advice in the essay chapters, you will take the philosophical path of writing about yourself first and then fitting your answers into the application rather than following the questions and forcing yourself inside the constraints of a particular question.

You may find that you have already specifically answered the first Common Application essay question, "Evaluate a significant experience, achievement, risk you have taken, or ethical dilemma you have faced and its impact on you." In that case, just check off that question and you're done. The problem with the second question, "Discuss some issue of personal, local, national, or international concern and its importance to you," is that it tends to provoke impersonal academic essays rather than personal accounts. Of course, it is possible to relate a major issue to you as a person, but it's very difficult to do without writing a book report on a national issue that leaves you out of the picture. For the most part, this question is not conducive to personal statements. A notable exception would be if you are from a contentious region of the world (Afghanistan, Somalia) and can relate a major international issue to you and your family. In that case, be sure to talk more about the impact on you and your family than the textbook details.

I would avoid the third essay at all costs, "Indicate a person who has had a significant influence on you and describe that influence." This question falls straight into one of Harry Bauld's clichéd essay categories. Even if you write a beautiful tribute to someone, what will the admissions committee learn about *you*? After all, you are the applicant, not your grandmother who survived the Holocaust or your father who helped you through rough times. Once again, there are ways to do this essay well (focusing more on how that person helped *you* through a personal issue and less on the particular person), but that leads to a somewhat artificial construct. The same goes for the fourth essay on a character in fiction, history, or a creative work. If you can address that question while talking mostly about yourself, feel free, but most students are not able to do so. The fifth topic, how you would add to the educational mix, is more like the personal supplemental essay I suggested you include, so save the thought.

That leaves choice number six, a topic of your choice, for which most students usually produce better essays. If you follow the essay chapter carefully, you'll find that your essay becomes a real personal statement, not just some canned response to a predetermined question. The college essay should not be restrictive; it should be liberating. If you don't feel liberated, ignore all the questions, write your personal essay, and then invent the question you could have responded to.

Other Required Information

Note two new checkboxes that are now included on the Common Application: (1) "Have you ever been found responsible for a disciplinary violation at any school you have attended, whether related to academic misconduct or behavioral misconduct, that resulted in your probation, suspension, removal, dismissal, or expulsion from the institution?"

and (2) "Have you ever been convicted of a misdemeanor, felony, or other crime?" It's important to tell the truth! These same questions appear on the school counselor form as well. The only thing worse than having committed any kind of violation would be lying about it. We can't undo the past, but we can at least provide the context for the violation. So take the time to write a note with a complete, honest, and detailed explanation of the circumstances surrounding the violation. Err on the side of honesty and culpability. Bear in mind that colleges are most concerned with academic violations (many colleges have strict honor codes) and violent outbursts that might put others in danger. If you were suspended for a minor peccadillo such as gum chewing or staying up after lights-out, don't panic; just document it. Admissions officers read your explanation with great care. If they have any questions, it's not unheard of for them to follow up with a phone call to the high school. Don't forget to sign the part below that says that your application is complete and you have presented all the information honestly.

An Important Note Regarding Typing Versus Handwriting

Most parents I have worked with are convinced that their children should type their applications or have them typeset by a professional so it looks neat. Keeping in mind that all the essays plus the activity list will be typed, I disagree. Sure, it may be neater to have your dad's secretary type in all your information, but the problem is that colleges usually think, "I bet the student had his mother or father's secretary type it for him." Therefore, I think there is some advantage to neatly printing the short-answer parts of the application yourself. Think of the advantages:

1. The application looks like it was completed by a real human being, making it less likely that you simply filled out one Common Application for twenty colleges.

2. Even if you have to use Wite-Out to correct some things (which is perfectly okay), you convey the I'm-a-real-student-and-I-make-small-mistakes ethos.

3. You prove that you did not use your advantaged background to have someone type the application for you.

Though it sounds counterintuitive, you may have a slight advantage by handwriting your application, and in the hyper-competitive world of college admissions, every little bit counts.

What about online applications? Unless a college requires one, use the old-fashioned way, filling out the form by hand. In our increasingly technologically oriented world, there is still some benefit to using pen and paper (heck, I'd use a quill if I could). It certainly does make it look more personal.

If you have horrible writing, type your answers on the computerized PDF file and then print it out rather than sending it electronically. While at first it seems easier to submit your whole application online, you'll find many small headaches, such as formatting issues and word limit problems, that make it easier to submit your application by mail.

Summary

1. Remember, most of the spaces in the Common Application will have "Please see attached." That's okay—that's why you did all the hard work on the essays in the first place.

2. Don't offer more information than you need to. Think of colleges as being on a need-to-know basis only; some things they just don't need to know.

3. Be truthful—there is an ethical difference between helping colleges focus on your achievements and outright lying. The latter will sink you quicker than lead in quicksand.

4. Handwrite the short responses if you have decent penmanship.

5. Don't forget to include the application fee. Leav-

ing it out will dramatically slow down the processing of your application.

6. Don't forget to sign and date the application.

7. Don't forget to include all your attachments *in the order they are asked for.*

8. Fill out all the requested information. Don't leave out your school's College Entry Examination Board (CEEB) code.

9. If you have AP or IB scores, be sure to write them in the Academic Honors section—include future AP classes here as well. Don't forget to send the official score reports in.

10. When including your essays, be sure to double- and triple-check that you have changed the name of the college. Nothing turns off a college faster than having a student say, "For all these reasons I think Duke is a perfect match for me," when you are applying to Davidson.

11. Remember to spell-check all your materials and have a literate person read over your application to make sure you haven't made any glaring typos.

12. One or two words crossed out are okay, but use Wite-Out if you need to, or simply download another copy of the application and do it over so it's neat.

ACING THE COLLEGE APPLICATION

13. When you mail your materials to the admissions office, use a service that provides tracking information so you can be sure your package arrived. (UPS, DHL, and FedEx are much more reliable than the U.S. Postal Service, which only lets you "look" for a lost package after thirty days.)

9

PUTTING IT ALL TOGETHER AND FOLLOWING UP

Once you have the various pieces of the puzzle gathered, your final task is to assemble them in an orderly fashion. Thanks to the computer, this job is not nearly as onerous as it used to be. For those who have mastered the "Save As" command on the computer, this should be the easy part. Let's take it step-by-step.

1. *The activity list.* Once you have completed the generic version of the activity list, you are done. You'll want to check and double-check spelling, grammar, and completeness, of course. But once you have signed off, just print off as many copies of the activity list as you have applications. There is no need to personalize the activity list. Every college will get a copy of this list just as it is. Final

check: Make sure you put in the header with your name, Social Security number, date of birth, and high school name so that information appears on every page.

2. *The main essay question.* The format will be the same for every essay question. First, create folders on your computer (using the "New Folder" command) for every school you are applying to. Next, take your generic main essay and add two pieces of information. On the top line, type the name of the college and then make it stand out (boldface, italics, underline, whatever you like) in the center. Then, space down and type in the exact question number and question phrasing used in that application—try setting this off in italics. The top of your personalized essay should now look like this:

Walla Walla University
Question 5. Detail your most embarrassing life moment from before age ten.

Once you've personalized the essay, use the "Save As" command and call this "Walla Walla Main Essay" and save it to the Walla Walla folder.

3. *The short essay questions.* The same rules apply— write the name of the school on top, the question underneath (*Question 3. Please elaborate on an ac-*

tivity . . .), and then save it to the folder for that college.

4. *The supplemental essay.* Even if a college doesn't specifically ask for a second essay, you might as well include it because you did such a good job writing it. Write the name of the school on the top as you did before and simply add the heading "Additional Essay" or "Supplemental Essay" or "Extra Essay." Colleges tend to read through your application, so even if they skim this essay, they will certainly see it. Using the "Save As" command, save the personalized version of your generic essay to the Walla Walla folder.

5. *Extra information.* If there are any other questions (sometimes there are lists of questions), you can simply type up the answers all on one page using the same format. Use a heading with your name, Social Security number, date of birth, and high school name, put the name of the college on the top, and then type in the question and your response right below it. Note that some colleges ask you to use the space provided and *not* to attach extra sheets. It's always a good idea to follow their directions, so be sure to read school-specific directions.

Students always get panicky about the order of the materials. The general rule of thumb is to put all the essays in the exact order in which the questions appear in the application.

Admissions officers have an incredible number of applications to get through each day and they are used to their own application's order and format. Don't invoke their wrath by messing up the system. Therefore, if the activity list is first, short answers second, main essay next, and extra essay plus your "why" paragraph last, you should put your sheets in that exact order. It really couldn't be more straightforward. The best thing to do is staple the activity sheet together, and then leave the other papers loose but in the proper order. Then, simply tuck the whole collection right into the middle of the application itself or below the last page of the Common Application if you used the printed copy. That way, when the admissions people are ready to read your file, everything will be, as Faulkner put it, in its ordered place.

The final issue is how to mail in the applications. The first point to consider is that the deadline always refers to the postmark deadline. Therefore, January 1 means you have to mail the application on or before January 1. Late students always ask me if they should rush to FedEx the materials if they are a day late. I say save your money—it takes admissions people two to four weeks to open, sort, date-stamp, and file all the applications, so no one will even see when your application was mailed. What actually happens is that admissions staff, secretaries, and anyone else who is free take shifts, rip open all the envelopes, date-stamp the documents, input them into the computer, and file them. It always pained me to see all those FedEx envelopes sit on the mailroom floor for weeks as we tried to keep up with the mail.

Don't make the admissions office's life difficult.* Imagine being on their end and having to sign for sixteen thousand packages in a three-week period. You can always track the package, even without a signature. Here's a final checklist that highlights some common mistakes students make before mailing off their applications:

1. Enclose the application check. Your application will not be read without it.

2. Make sure every piece of loose paper has a header with your name, Social Security number, date of birth, and high school name on it.

3. Make sure your application is written neatly and legibly.

4. Make sure you've written "Please see attached essay" in every blank on the form so that the admissions officers know that you, in fact, answered the question.

5. Check to see that you've included copies of all the essays they've asked for and maybe one or two extras, including your "why" paragraph.

---

*Although you should use a tracking method, make sure to waive any delivery signature.

6. Check that you've signed and dated in all the appropriate places.

7. Double-check that all the Amherst College essays say Amherst College on top and that you've included the Amherst "why" paragraph.

8. Be sure to send official score reports for the SAT I and II, AP/IB tests, and the ACT if you took it.

10

TEACHER AND COUNSELOR RECOMMENDATIONS

Although the section numbering differs from application to application, almost all colleges want one or two teacher recommendations. Every college requires the secondary school report (i.e., the high school transcript) and an official letter from the college counselor. Those forms are included as part of your application packet. If you are using the Common Application, be sure to photocopy the teacher recommendation form. Unless a particular college stresses outright that you need only one teacher recommendation, you should send in two. If you need extra teacher recommedation forms, print out additional copies.

Teacher recommendations are among the most important parts of your application. No matter how strong you look from your materials, colleges will look to your teachers to second what you say about yourself. If you tout yourself as a history genius but your history teacher rates you as only average, you have just shot yourself in the foot. The first thing my students usually ask me is whether they should ask a teacher known as a good writer or one who adores them. Forget the teacher's writing ability. Admissions officers read these letters so quickly that the last thing they are focusing on is the teacher's writing ability. Besides, they are not going to reward or punish you based on your teacher's grammatical skills. They are looking for substance: your passion for the subject, what kind of student you are, if you go above and beyond the basic requirements, your intellectual capacity, how you compare to your classmates and how you compare to the top students that teacher has taught during his career. Ask the teacher who knows you best and has seen your best work. Don't just ask the teacher everyone asks—that doesn't make sense anyway because if a teacher is swamped, he or she will not have the time to write with the appropriate level of detail. In general, it's a good idea to request one from an English/writing teacher, because all colleges, even those with technical specialities, are concerned with students' writing ability.

Even if your ninth-grade teacher adored you, don't ask for a recommendation—it's past its prime. If you get past teachers to write your recommendations, admissions officers will assume that you had no teachers you could turn to from eleventh and twelfth grades. Besides, it's not until eleventh or twelfth grade that most students take upper-level courses. Colleges want to read recommendations from teachers who have taught courses that are close to college level. It's a good idea to ask one teacher from eleventh grade and one of your teachers from twelfth grade. If you are unsure of whom to ask, sometimes it's a good idea to ask your guidance counselor. I say that because at well-organized schools, savvy guidance counselors often ask teachers to write brief one-paragraph descriptions of all students so that the counselor can excerpt from these passages when writing the official letter. In this case, the counselor would be able to render a professional judgment about who actually did praise you the most highly.

There are many etiquette faux pas that students make, so let's go over some fundamentals of courtesy and good manners. First of all, when asking teachers to write a letter of recommendation, be sure you give them a graceful escape route—if they indicate that they wouldn't feel comfortable writing a letter, don't push it. They are trying to tell you that they don't have anything nice to say. Try something like this: "Mr. X, I am applying for early decision to Northwestern and I wanted to ask you if you feel you know me well enough to write a strong letter of recommendation." There, you've given teacher X a perfect way to either graciously accept or decline your offer. By adding "strong," you've made him consider whether he thinks you are one of his top students. If he doesn't think so, you don't want him to write your letter. Ask your teachers to focus on your academics, not your personality. I read literally thousands of teacher recommendations in my four seasons of admissions reading; sometimes I was surprised that so many teachers took the opportunity to tell us how nice Rachel was, or what a great piano player she was. Teachers should focus almost exclusively on your academic achievements and your intellectual merit. Competitive colleges will assume you're a nice person, but niceness alone never got anyone into college. I wouldn't make such a major point of this except for the fact that I read so many poor teacher recommendations.

The other mistake teachers make is to be too long-winded. I'd rather see a short letter that said something like, "I've been teaching AP physics for twenty-five years and I can say without a doubt that James is one of the most brilliant minds in physics that I've come across. It's rare to find someone his age who uses such an intuitive problem-solving method. All his classmates regard him with awe—he even surprises me at times." In just a few sentences, this teacher has conveyed the precise information the admissions office needs: This student is a standout, not just among this year's class but among twenty-five years of top students. No need to ramble on and on. Admissions officers skim teacher recommendations to find out (1) the student's level of intellectual ability, (2) the student's level of passion, (3) how the student compares to others in the class, and (4) how the student compares to other students the teacher has taught. Anything beyond this is usually unnecessary.

What can you do to make sure your teachers don't go overboard describing your personality? Try the direct route: "Thank you so much for agreeing to write my college recommendation. The colleges I'm applying to are very competitive and stress that they want teachers to focus on academic excellence. I'd really appreciate it if you could give them a good idea of what I'm like as a math student in your class." How could that offend a teacher? It only helps them concentrate on what is essential. Of course, they can mention that you are also the top leader in your school, but they don't need to elaborate. They *do* need to elaborate on your academic talents, papers you have written, your class participation, your ability, and your intellectual firepower.

As a teacher myself for many years, I get the feeling that students don't appreciate how busy teachers are. It's a big favor to ask your teacher to write you a recommendation, so be respectful and do everything you can to make life easier. Remember, it's always the best teachers who are asked to write the most recommendations, and they don't get paid extra for their efforts. How can you do this? First, be sure to fill out all the biographical information on the top of the recommendation form. As much as your teacher adores you, he doesn't want to waste time filling in your name and personal information, which you probably know a lot better than he does. Second, be sure to provide a stamped, self-addressed envelope. I still can't get over how many students leave out this step. Teachers are not millionaires. The most popular ones write upward of twenty-five letters every fall—that's a lot of postage, especially considering that some schools do not include this postage allowance in their budgets. Plus, they don't have the time to fill out a return address or to look up the address. You do not want to do anything that will distract them from their primary task of writing the letter. Ideally, they fill out the checklist, print out a copy of the letter, and then simply place it into the envelope you provided and drop it right in the mail. Third, don't ask them the day before the letters are due. Show some respect. Better to have your materials prepared ahead of time, especially if you are applying for early decision or early action. Even if the application is not due until January 1, it's never too early. For early decision, I'd aim to give them the forms in September or early October. For regular decision (because they will have to write more than one), October is not too early. At least that way teachers can plan their schedules accordingly.

When you ask a teacher to write the letter, be sure to stress how much you appreciate it. Do not simply say, "Here's my letter—I want you to write it." Remember, the teacher is doing you a favor! Finally, after a sufficient amount of time (after you are sure the teacher has mailed the letter, so there is no conflict of interest), buy the teacher a small present that shows your appreciation, such as a Borders or Starbucks gift card, or at the very least write a nice note. These are the kinds of gestures that teachers remember years later. Be considerate of their time and show your appreciation.

If you are applying early but know that if you don't get in you will be applying to more schools, ask the teacher whether he prefers to do all the letters at once or whether he wants to do the early one (and save the letter on his computer) and wait before doing the others. That way you are giving him the chance to organize his own time. Also, you are reminding him to keep a letter on the computer so that he can simply print out more copies for your other schools. Only the individual teacher knows her schedule, so leave the decision to her. By offering to give her all the forms early, you are making it easier for her to plan her fall.

The guidance counselor letter is a bit different. It is the counselor's responsibility to provide all the official information: the difficulty of your course load; any disciplinary incidents; your GPA, class rank, and grades; your transcript; and how you compare to your classmates. You don't need to tell the counselor what to stress because he or she should know by now. For students who attend large schools (either public or private), take the time to meet with your counselor early in the fall. Unfortunately, many big urban public schools assign as many as five hundred students to one counselor. Obviously, these counselors do not have the time to write detailed letters. Help them out. Meet briefly with your counselor (if nothing else so he or she knows you by name), bring your completed materials (the activity list will help the counselor summarize your activities and school leadership) with you, and tell him or her which schools you are applying to and why. That way the counselor can reaffirm your interest in your top-choice schools. Don't assume that your counselor knows you well. Even counselors who have to write only a handful of letters usually don't teach students themselves, so they don't have a firsthand sense of what particular students are like in class.

No counselor worth her salt should mind that you are taking the time to go over your main academic and extracurricular activities. In reality, you are making life much easier for her. Because the high school is responsible for expenses in the case of the guidance counselor letter, you do not have to pay postage. There are some exceptions even here: If the school is running late or you are apprehensive about using the mail, offer to pay the extra money for FedEx, UPS, or DHL. Often the school will budget in the extra cost, but it's polite to offer to pay if you want expedited delivery.

The teacher recommendations and the official school recommendation are two of the most important components of your application. It's worth taking extra time to get to know your teachers and counselor, to do everything you can to make their lives easier by filling out forms and providing stamped self-addressed envelopes, and to make sure that they feel comfortable writing your recommendations. Many students spend an inordinate amount of time on their part of the application but give no thought to the teacher and counselor recommendations. Considering their importance, not paying attention could be a fatal mistake. Take the time to do this part correctly—you won't be sorry you did.

11
THE OPTIONAL PEER RECOMMENDATION

Only a handful of colleges ask for a letter written by a peer (Dartmouth being one of them), so I won't spend too much time on this section. Why would a college ask for a peer recommendation in the first place? Unlike teachers and guidance counselors, friends tend to write more sincerely and more personally about what a student is really like. I have to admit that I often found peer references quite helpful in rounding out a student's portrait. Even though I stressed that teachers should focus only on academic areas, it's perfectly okay for friends to mention personal traits and leadership qualities. Overall, the most helpful information is the most specific. Ask your friend to provide some detail. Vague or general descriptions do little to add to a student's profile. Your friends know better than your teachers what you really do in your spare time.

Like any other recommendation, the peer recommendation should confirm what the admissions office has already been able to find out by reading your file. If you write all about your obsession with astronomy and telescopes and your friend writes that he can't believe you stand outside in the freezing cold in winter to get a good view of the heavens, that would provide solid backup to points brought up elsewhere in the application. In this case, your teachers may not know about your obsession, but your friends will. While your friend should provide details about meaningful things you do, they would do well to avoid the nights you spent on typically teenage things that could get you in trouble. It's certain that most teens do some activities they oughtn't, but the admissions office doesn't really need to know. I only mention it because sometimes friends feel they are confessors who have to turn in their friends for some minor peccadillo—not a good idea. The admissions office does not need to hear of any teenage misadventures unless there is a point that relates to intellect.

In most cases, some nice personal stories about what you're like (especially how you're viewed in your school) will be the most helpful. It's nice to hear from a friend that you are regarded with awe by your physics class because you are a total science genius. That kind of anecdote is sure to impress an admissions office. Or that most people don't know how you rescue stray dogs in your spare time—a few specific instances will suffice for the peer recommendation.

To summarize, the sole purpose of a peer recommendation is to flesh out the application in a little more detail or to round out a profile. You should include one only if the college requests it. Specificity helps quite a bit here. Friends should write from the heart and focus on your intellectual talents, hobbies, and main interests or passions.

12
THE INTERVIEW

THE ON-CAMPUS INTERVIEW

There are two totally different types of interviews at most colleges, the on-campus interview and the alumni interview. In general, the smaller liberal arts colleges offer on-campus interviews. Dartmouth announced in 2007 they would no longer do on-campus interviews, so the only Ivy League college to offer on-campus interviews to anyone is Yale. Stanford and MIT do not do on-campus interviews either. Penn and Columbia offer on-campus interviews only to those whose parents or grandparents attended. Most of the smaller schools *do* offer on-campus interviews. The easiest way to distinguish between them relates to the timing. An on-campus interview must take place roughly between the end of May and September of the summer before twelfth grade because colleges have neither the time nor the resources to interview students before that time frame. Alumni interviews take place from November to February of your *senior* year after you have already applied. As the name indicates, on-campus interviews happen on the college campus, while an alumni interview occurs in your hometown.

Let's look at the on-campus interview first. Even if you were a motivated high school freshman, an admissions office would not agree to interview you until you were finishing up your junior year. Most students never get to this point because it takes quite a bit of planning in terms of travel, schedule coordination, and free time. But if you are really interested in a school, taking the initiative to set up a campus visit and an interview is an excellent way to show your interest and sincerity in applying to that school. If you can call the admissions office and arrange for your interview in late June or July, you will be much better off than saving it until August. First of all, the same small handful of admissions officers and student interviewers interview up to six students a day, every day, from late June until August, so you can imagine how bored and tired they are of interviewing by the time August comes around. Second, admissions offices are zoos in August because this is the season that most students and their parents seem to get around to visiting colleges. Therefore, it is definitely to your advantage to set up an early interview and get it over with as soon as possible. You'll have to call each admissions office to find out their exact schedules, but usually if you call around the end of May or early June you will be able to set up an interview in June or July. Because there are a limited number of slots, schedule early.

The first major point to keep in mind is that in 90 percent of the cases, an interview helps the student. This alone should prevent you from getting nervous or intimidated. The whole raison d'être behind the interview is to help the admissions office get to know you better and to match their observations with what teachers and guidance counselors say about you. The admissions office won't actually look at the interview write-up until the official admissions season, at which point the interview will be read in the context of your entire application. There are many misconceptions and myths about these interviews that simply aren't true.

 ## TEN COMMON MYTHS AND MISCONCEPTIONS

1. *If you are shy, you should skip the interview.* This is just plain wrong! The interviewer is trying to see how deep your passions lie, how committed you are, how smart you are, and how motivated you are. There are plenty of shy students who light up when talking about subjects that interest them. If you are a bit shy, don't be so nervous—the burden is on the interviewer to put you at ease and try to get the best from you. If you prepare for the interview, there is really nothing to be nervous about.

2. *The more charming you are, the higher your rating.* Although it doesn't hurt to be charming, there are certain points the interviewer is looking for. Substance is more important than superficial personality. This means that even very sociable students should think carefully about the major points they want to get across in the interview.

3. *Interviews are very formal and you should wear a dress or a suit.* Remember, it will be summer and a suit is a bit much. If you show up too dressed up, the admissions staff will think it's to try to cover up any lack of real depth or character. There are some exceptions—if a school is extremely traditional, you may be able to wear a more formal outfit. The best strategy is to ask the receptionist or secretary on the phone how most students dress. For the most part, you don't want to be too conspicuous either way—not too formal, not too casual. For boys, khaki pants and a neat polo or button-down shirt with dress shoes is perfectly fine, while girls can wear neat slacks or a skirt and a shirt or blouse. To avoid underdressing, try to stay away from jeans or athletic-looking sneakers. Because you never know who will interview you and what his or her personal prejudices are, it's probably best to take out your nose ring, lip ring, or multiple piercings.

4. *Interviewers want to intimidate you.* To the contrary, they want to make you comfortable: That is their job. There are always some inept interviewers or those who pride themselves on being intimidating, but they are few and far between.

5. *A short interview is bad and a long interview is good.* Though in general this can be true, a lot depends on how busy the interviewer's schedule is. If he has only an hour slot for you (and it will take him fifteen minutes to write up the interview once you leave) and he has another interview the next hour, the interview won't go much over thirty minutes because he'll need to write yours up before the next student arrives. (They have to visit the bathroom every once in a while, too.) A good interviewer can get quite a lot of information in only twenty minutes.

6. *You shouldn't say anything controversial.* Most students are scared to say anything negative about their school or their classes—to voice a dissenting opinion. Unfortunately, this makes many interviews quite boring. Obviously, you don't want to say that you think the Holocaust never happened or that you believe in slavery, but other than truly offensive and ignorant opinions, you absolutely *should*

state your position honestly and directly. Otherwise, the interview will be cookie-cutter boring.

7. *If the interviewer asks a question you can't answer, you are ruined.* Not at all! The best answer to a question you absolutely don't know is, "That's an excellent question but I have to admit I don't know" or "I'd have to give that one a little more thought." Admitting you don't know is better than faking it or making something up. Remember the famous "euthanasia" mistake when a student answered, "I'm not sure about the youth in Asia, but I think the youth in America . . ."

8. *It's bad to ask the interviewer pointed questions about the school.* Actually, most interviewers will tell you that the purpose of the interview is twofold: to get to know you, and for you to find out more about the school. This latter part indicates that a major reason for the interview is for you to be able to ask questions. Be sure to do your research ahead of time so you'll be prepared.

9. *If the interviewer is very encouraging, your interview went well.* Not necessarily. It is their job to make sure that everyone feels the interview went well. I can remember interviews where I was very unimpressed with the student, but I still had to go through the motions of thanking him or her for coming and I'd still go downstairs to say hi to the

student's parents. Part of the interview is market-
ing the school, so no professional interviewer
should make you feel that the interview was a di-
saster, even if it was.

10. *If the interview is unfriendly or businesslike, the interview
    went badly.* Again, not so. Many interviewers try to
    remain poker-faced even when they are truly im-
    pressed. Don't judge your interview by a superficial
    reaction. The real measure comes later when the
    interviewer sits down to write up the interview.

 HOW TO PREPARE FOR THE INTERVIEW

Though you don't need to spend weeks preparing, like anything else in life, being prepared does help. Keeping in mind
that you will be judged roughly 70 percent on academics
and 30 percent on personal and extracurricular activities
combined, you should try to devote roughly that percentage
to your answers. It's not an exact science, of course, but if
you spend the entire forty-five minutes talking about your
love of rock climbing, the interviewer will have to assume
that you don't care much about academics. From my experience interviewing at Dartmouth College for four years, I'd
say this is the number one mistake made by students. They
fall all over themselves trying to show their leadership or
their talents when they should have devoted more time to
their scholarly side. As a general rule of thumb, the more se-

lective the college, the more they will be interested first and foremost in your academic strengths.

To prepare mentally, sit down, look over your activity sheet, think about the essays you wrote for your application, and make a list of the two or three most important facets of your intellectual interests and the two or three most important facets of your leadership or extracurricular pursuits. Keep it simple—you will not have time to cover everything in your interview and you may get off on a tangent (which is fine), but at a bare minimum, you want to make sure to cover these basic points. Think long and hard about what your most salient academic and extracurricular strengths are and memorize them. Once you know the main points you want to stress, the interviewer's questions become almost irrelevant.

Let's say you are dying to talk about the research paper you did on the causes of World War I because it was a major project that took you two months of your junior year. The problem is, the interviewer has not asked about any major projects. Now it's your job to direct your answer from a different topic. No problem. "John, tell me a little bit about your course load last year and this year." Rather than rattling off every course, list a few and then weave in your paper: "Last year I took a very difficult course load of four APs, but I have to say that history was my absolute favorite. I got a little carried away by the junior year history project and ended up writing a twenty-page paper on the causes of World

War I. Once I realized the intricate balance of power in Europe right before the assassination of the Archduke Ferdinand, I decided to explore in depth the various causes. My research showed me that . . ." By the time you get into some detail, the interviewer should be caught up in the excitement, not sitting there saying, "But what were your other classes?" You can always return to the original question when you're done but it's better that you took the time to show some intellectual depth.

The interviewer would prefer not to have to sit there and ask you hundreds of questions to keep you talking. That's why you should feel free to take a question and run with it. Imagine the situation from the interviewer's side. A student in his office answers every question with a short answer (Q: "What is your school like?" A: "It's pretty good, academically speaking.") Rather than listening to the student's responses, he has to sit there thinking of the next question to avoid that awkward silence. Don't let this happen to you. Feel free to get a little carried away. Remember our watchwords, "passion" and "initiative." By elaborating in great detail about projects you have done, notable essays or major papers, experiments, research, et cetera, you are showing your academic passion. Again, from my experience, most students make the mistake of not providing enough detail. Don't wait for the interviewer to ask you something. Feel free to volunteer it, "In fact, now that I'm on the topic of history, I should add that I competed on my school's nationally competitive debate club. This year's debate actually focused on another aspect of World War I, so the research I did on my paper allowed me to beat my opponents."

In a perfect interview, the interviewer may ask only a few general questions and hope you'll fill in the rest. Remember, be vivid, give particulars, and don't be afraid to go into some depth and detail. Remember that every interviewer has a different style. Some ask lots of short questions, while some prefer to ask only one general one like, "So, Sarah, tell me about your school." In the event of a general question like this, you can see how helpful your mental list is. Rather than dreading such a general question, you should be mentally cheering that the ball is now in your court. You can probably get all of your major points in during the first ten minutes, and then the rest of the interview is the whipped cream on the sundae.

Along with mental preparation, you want to do some research on the school you are visiting. No student should show up for an on-campus interview without having a pretty detailed reading knowledge of the school. One great resource is the campus newspaper—read the last few issues online before your interview so you are aware of all the latest campus news and controversies. One question you absolutely should be prepared to answer is why you are interested in that particular school. During the interview, they may judge you quite strictly on your interest and knowledge of the school. This is not the time to spout general statistics, such as "I want to go to your school because of the excellent faculty/student ratio." They hear that all the time. Try to personalize your reason for attending, "As you can see from my record, I've been interested in engineering since I was fifteen years old. I like the fact that your engineering program is a distinct major, not a separate school. I've spoken to several students at your school who highlight the noncompetitive nature of the program, which sets it apart from other more stressful programs I've read about. After I read about the annual race car competition, I knew this was going to be my top choice." Now that's a well-thought-out answer. The student has clearly done his research.

Beware trying to fake this information. Do your homework. At Dartmouth, I'd have students say things like, "I want to major in business at Dartmouth," which is not a good thing to say because there is no undergraduate business major. Others would say things like, "I want to get into Dartmouth's law school," which would be great except for the fact that there is no law school. Don't get caught mentioning a major that doesn't exist or a program that isn't there because it will take away from all the positive points of your interview.

Finally, be natural and relaxed (easier said than done). It's perfectly normal to be jittery right before your interview, and a little bit of nervousness will keep you on your toes and sharpen your mind. As long as you have a general idea of what you want to get across, there is nothing the interviewer can do to derail you. Keep in mind that your interviewer is just a regular person, not a monster. Most of the interviewers on summer staff are actually current seniors at the school who are trained to do this (without them, colleges would not be able to interview more than a small percentage of applicants). There is really no major difference between having an admissions officer or a student do the interview. A student may make you feel more at ease. In any case, the interview is weighted exactly the same. Our director at Dartmouth used to say to alumni parents who would try to get him as the interviewer: "That may not be a good idea because if I'm not impressed, the interview may have a stronger weight than you want it to have."

You should look forward to your interviews rather than dreading them. In this positive frame of mind, you will be much better positioned to take advantage of this one-on-one time to showcase your talents. It's your chance to strut your stuff—use it!

Now for a few final reminders and some practical issues to keep in mind. It's often a good idea to bring a copy of your activity list. Just in case the interviewer does not want to see it (some prefer not to), be sure to leave him a graceful way out, "If it helps you, I've brought along a copy of my activity list in case we don't have time to touch on all of my various leadership positions. If you'd like a copy, I'd be happy to leave it with you." That way, the interviewer can either accept it or say that he prefers to cover just a smaller segment of your talents in the interview. At the end of the interview, ask for the interviewer's card so you can write him a thank-you note when you get home. Even senior interviewers will either have cards or a premade address sheet. Although this is not mandatory and won't get you in, it is a nice courtesy. Like many things in life, it's more noticeable by its absence than by its presence. Keep it brief.

Dear Mr. X,

Thanks so much for taking the time to interview me on July 5. I really enjoyed our conversation, especially our shared love of old Humphrey Bogart films.

Sincerely,

By mentioning something specific, the interviewer will at least remember who you are. After doing five or six interviews a day, it gets pretty hard to keep students straight, even if you really like someone. Finally, write out a list of specific questions before your interview because every interviewer will ask at some point, "Do you have any questions?" Avoid easy factual questions that can be looked up. As a table-turning strategy, I always encourage students to put the interviewer on the spot by asking tough questions. If he is going to have the audacity to test you, I think you should have the right to make him work. The students I was most impressed by put the burden on me to prove that Dartmouth should be interested in them, not vice versa.

Let me give you some real examples of interview questions I heard at Dartmouth from some very impressive students:

1. "I'm trying to decide between Dartmouth and Yale. One thing that concerns me about Dartmouth is that some of the professors I've spoken to complain that the ten-week trimesters do not allow enough time for in-depth exploration. Did you find that to be a problem in your experience?"

A question such as this shows that the student has taken the time to actually speak to Dartmouth professors. Talk about doing your homework! Plus, the message is clear: This student felt he was a good candidate for both Yale and Dartmouth. This shifts the responsibility to the interviewer, who by now wants this student to come to Dartmouth, not a rival such as Yale. It was then my turn to defend Dartmouth's trimester system. Very clever.

2. "I've been looking mostly at engineering programs and I'm concerned that Dartmouth only allows undergraduates to major in engineering. How do your engineering majors stack up to those at more technological schools such as MIT and Caltech?"

Again, zing, what a good question! A heck of a lot better than, "How many students does Dartmouth have?" To that, I'd be tempted to say, "Why don't you look it up?"

3. "My high school's social life was dominated by the jocks. I'm looking for a college with a much more

intellectual atmosphere than my high school. I know Dartmouth's party reputation is a bit outdated, but can you give me some specific examples of what the administration is doing at Dartmouth to encourage intellectual discussion?"

This is much more thoughtful than the usual, "Is it true that Dartmouth is a big drinking school?"

4. "What opportunities are there for upperclassmen to work one-on-one with professors in senior projects or theses?"

Again, this question shows that the student is looking at specific aspects of every college, not just the class size or teacher-student ratio.

Take some time to construct some thoughtful questions that pertain to your own interests, both academic and extracurricular. Don't be caught with nothing at all to ask. In the best of cases, prove to the interviewer that she should be begging you to apply to the school. If you can succeed at this, the interview will have served even more than its primary purpose of fleshing out your application in more detail.

THE ALUMNI INTERVIEW

Everything we've said about the on-campus interview in terms of doing your homework and preparing questions is also true for the alumni interview. There are only a few differences I'd like to emphasize.

Unlike the majority of admissions officers, alumni interviewers are graduates of that particular college. What you won't know until you meet them is if they are recent graduates or old graduates.

As a general rule, alumni lean toward being more conservative than their admissions counterparts, or may dress the part if they are interviewing you at their office, so you may want to dress a little neater than normal. If they are meeting you on a Sunday for coffee, you can be more casual. Alumni usually do not have five interviews scheduled in a row, so you may have the chance for a longer interview or be able to discuss topics more in-depth. It's to your advantage to establish what we referred to earlier as a bond of commonality between you and your interviewers. This means that if you have any favorite books, movies, directors, academic disciplines, or hobbies, try to mention as many as you can. The odds are good that you will find some common bond. There is nothing an alumni interviewer enjoys more than meeting a young person with a similar interest, be it golf or spy novels. I remember interviewing a student who loved completing two-thousand-piece jigsaw puzzles, a hobby that occupied me for years. Of course, I instantly liked this student and wanted to have a more in-depth conversation with him.

As a general rule, alumni—really, just about anyone—enjoy talking about themselves, so feel free to ask them about their specific experiences at the college when it's your turn to ask questions.

1. "You've mentioned that you're an American history buff, too. Did you major in history? How did you find the professors in that department?"

2. As we did in the on-campus interview, it's often a good strategy to put him on the defensive about his school. "I'm interested in hearing what you think of the fraternity situation: I'm seriously considering Dartmouth and Princeton, but I've heard that the fraternity system has been under fire recently for inappropriate and sexist behavior—did you find this to be a problem when you were a student?" By wording the question this way, you are taking control of the interview and imparting the subtle message that you think you'd get into both Princeton and Dartmouth and are trying to decide between them.

As far as setting up the interview is concerned, once you have mailed in part one of your application (the part with the data and personal information), colleges send your information along to regional alumni representatives. One thing to keep in mind is that many regions have no alumni, so you will not even be offered an interview. The alumni interview network is completely dependent on volunteers. If you live in New York City, chances are good that there will be many alumni there to schedule an interview with you, but if you live in Utah, you may find yourself with no alums nearby. Don't worry if you cannot have an alumni interview. For your top-choice schools, I do recommend trying to set up one interview (either on-campus or alumni), but if you absolutely cannot, it's not worth losing sleep over. In fact, the majority of applicants do not have any kind of interview. As I mentioned at the start of the chapter, having an interview usually helps your application, but not having one does not hurt your chances.

If you have the good fortune of having both alumni and on-campus interviews, your odds of admission are slightly better because (1) the college knows you are seriously interested and (2) they will know more about you than they do about other students with no interviews. Unless an interview went badly, you will be at a distinct advantage.

A final caution about alumni interviewers—unlike admissions officers, they are not usually trained at giving interviews. Hence, it is quite possible that you will have a bad interviewer. Don't let it worry you. His lack of skill has nothing to do with you. That's why if you do your homework and are prepared to talk about your strengths, you can still get them across no matter what questions he asks you. By taking the reins during an interview, you will be doing a poor interviewer a favor. There are always stories, many greatly exaggerated, about alumni who were offensive, rude, mean, or disinterested. What should you do if something horrible happens during an alumni interview? If you are really worried about it, simply type out a brief note to the admissions office recounting your experience. Chances are, they are already aware of a crackpot interviewer. We had several I can recall from my years at Dartmouth. The trouble is, admissions offices are reluctant to "fire" volunteer interviewers for fear of offending them. Often they don't do anything about the person, but they do disregard the interview. Make them aware of the problem by writing a short note. No need to be offensive, just stick to the facts:

Dear X,

I am writing to alert you about one of your alumni interviewers, John Doe, who interviewed me on December 29. I was taken aback that he asked me several times about my religious ties and seemed offended when I told him I don't go to church on a weekly basis. To make matters worse, when I tried to tell him about my classes, he kept interrupting me to tell stories of the good old days at your school. I was very frustrated since he didn't give me a chance to talk about my own accomplishments. Thank you for your time.

Sincerely,

After reading a letter like this, the admissions office will be forced to discount the alumni interview and would probably feel sorry that you had to go through that. In some way, you'd probably get a more comprehensive reading than other applicants because of your traumatic experience.

As in the on-campus interview, ask for a business card so you can jot a thank-you note. Don't be surprised if the alum spends a great deal of time reminiscing about his college years. That's okay—most loyal alums love their college and are anxious to communicate that enthusiasm to all students they interview. The one thing that seems to offend alumni interviewers more than anything else is a student who does not know anything about the school: "Can you tell me if X has a nursing program?" Don't ask these kinds of basic questions at the risk of offending the alums, who are going to assume that you did your homework.

Overall, in any interview, keep the following points in mind:

1. Dress neatly, but don't overdo it.

2. Look the interviewer in the eye—looking down at your lap is not conducive to good two-way communication. And give a firm handshake—no one likes a wet noodle.

3. Avoid far-out expressions of your innermost self, such as tattoos, body piercings, or bright green hair.

4. Do feel free to voice your opinions if they are well thought out and you can defend them. No one wants a totally bland and sanitized response—take a stand.

5. Do write a thank-you note to be polite, but don't expect that it will get you in.

6. Do make a list of the two or three major academic topics and the two or three extracurricular interests you want to get across no matter what the interviewer asks you.

7. Do make sure you do your homework about the school and have a few thoughtful questions. Feel free to refer to your own notes for this part of the interview.

8. Do put the interviewer in the position of defending or explaining some aspect of the school that you are concerned about.

9. Do feel free to mention any odd hobbies, passions, or pursuits that float your boat. If you're lucky, you might establish that elusive bond of commonality.

10. Don't mumble or talk into your hands—speak up so the interviewer can hear you.

11. Don't worry if you're shy—focus on your strengths and substance and don't worry so much about the delivery.

12. Do bring a copy of your activity list, but don't assume that everyone will want it.

13. Keep in mind that by design the interview is structured to help your chances of admission by finding out more about you. Take advantage.

14. Do elaborate upon your answers. Remember, short, monosyllabic responses will not get you very far.

15. Overall, be sure you spend enough time on your academic interests. Because you will be judged first and foremost on your academics, don't make the mistake of speaking about your extracurricular activities for 90 percent of the interview. This is the most common mistake made by students. You can never spend too much time on academic interests.

The following is a short list of the fifteen most common interview questions I heard during my admissions experience:

1. Tell us about your school and your classes this year.

2. What do you do in your spare time?

3. Describe your most influential or favorite teacher.

4. Tell us about a book you read recently.

5. Is there any major project or research paper you are particularly proud of?

6. What has been your most exciting intellectual experience?

7. What are you looking for in your college experience? Why do you like our school?

8. What will be your biggest contributions to our campus?

9. Do you have any special talents or hobbies?

10. What would your favorite teacher say about you?

11. What do you see yourself doing in twenty years?

12. If you could change one thing about your high school, what would you change?

13. What would you do with a free day?

14. How would you want to be remembered?

15. Do you have questions for me?

13

EARLY ACTION VERSUS EARLY DECISION—THE TRADE-OFFS

In this chapter we will look at early decision and early action programs. As the admissions process has become more competitive, more students have realized that early plans maximize their chance of admission. As this chapter was being written, however, a few large schools (Harvard, Princeton, and the University of Virginia) have abolished their early programs in an (misguided, if you ask me) attempt to be more open to minority and low-income applicants. More on this aspect once I've explained the programs.

First, let's distinguish between the two most common early plans: early decision and early action. Early decision applications are usually due November 1 of senior year (some are due the tenth or fifteenth) *and are binding*. For the student, this means that if you can narrow your choices down to one school and you apply under early decision, you must attend the college if you are admitted. Naturally, this creates a great deal of pressure for students who are considering more than one college and have no clear front-runner. It also means that they have to plan much further ahead because all SAT I and SAT II testing should be close to complete. The November SAT I and IIs are too late for early decision—even the mid-October date cuts it very close. In fact, starting in 2006–7, the College Board for the first time, because of the scoring problems earlier in the year, will *not* have the October tests back to students until two to three weeks after the early deadlines, a major inconvenience. Selective colleges usually require the SAT I or the ACT and then two or three SAT II tests. To submit a series of top scores, students who apply early will need to start taking these tests as early as freshman or sophomore year to complete a full complement of testing.

Early action is similar to early decision in every way except for one key point: The decision *is not binding*. If you are accepted under an early action plan, you have a feather in your cap that you can hold on to until May if you wish, while you apply to a bunch of other colleges. The problem is that it is very difficult for colleges to predict their yield for early action—only Harvard can count on a yield close to 80 percent for early action, while other schools vary widely.

Recently, a few colleges have used an even more restrictive option called "single-choice early action" (SCEA), which is just like early action (nonbinding) except you cannot apply to ANY OTHER COLLEGE early decision or early action. In my view this is unfair to students. At a true early action college such as the University of Chicago, you are allowed to apply both early action to their school and early decision to another school with the understanding that if you get accepted to the early decision school, you are bound to accept their offer and immediately withdraw your application from the early action school. Some schools, most notably Georgetown, call themselves early action schools, but on their applications they expressly prohibit you from applying to any other early program, so they are in effect single-choice early action—no wonder parents and students are confused! The next few years will be a time of transition as colleges decide whether their early policies are viable. Stay tuned.

Many colleges in recent years have switched from early action to early decision. There is no doubt that the latter option is better for colleges because they know exactly who will make up the percentage of the class they decide to accept early. In effect, it takes the guesswork out of early action, a policy that yields few clues as to which students will accept the offer of admission. Brown University is the most recent Ivy League convert. In 2001, they changed their long-time early action policy to a binding early decision policy. In reality, there are only a handful of colleges that still have early action. Ten years ago you would have found many more. The main colleges that retain early action are Georgetown, the University of Chicago, Caltech, Notre Dame, Boston College, Yale (which is technically SAEA), and MIT. Just about every other college that has an early program has an early decision plan. Sometimes applying to a rolling-admissions college will yield quick results. Both the University of Michigan and the University of Wisconsin have rolling admissions policies, although the University of Michigan announced in 2007 that they would abandon their rolling policy for 2007–8 onward. Brandeis, for example, has a January 1 early decision deadline. But if you complete your application by November 15, Brandeis will give you a decision in four weeks. According to the admissions office there, the earlier a student applies, the better his chances. For the most updated list of all early decision/early action colleges and their respective time-tables, visit the College Board's site at www.collegeboard.com.

How is it possible that colleges insist on one hand that they do not want to see a harried rush of early applicants while on the other hand they accept such a tremendous number of applicants early? Anyone reading the statistics would be hard pressed *not* to be pressured into applying early. Though these numbers are hard to come by and colleges don't like you to see them, let's compare the early decision acceptance rate versus the regular acceptance rate at a few colleges for the class of 2011. At Yale, about 20 percent were accepted early, while only 6 percent of the regular applicants were accepted. That means that students had a better than triple chance of acceptance by applying early than by waiting until regular acceptance. It also means that a student applying for early decision to Yale has close to a 20 percent chance of getting in, whereas if she waits until regular acceptance, her odds are next to impossible. Similarly, at Columbia, 24 percent of the early candidates are accepted compared to a mere 8.5 percent of regular, and Princeton accepted 26 percent early and only 7 percent for regular. To look at a more recent admissions year, here is a chart of the early acceptance rate and the regular decision acceptance rate for those colleges that provide this information.

Looking at these statistics, one has to disregard what colleges say about not rushing to apply early. Although I don't agree that students should have to have a definite first choice school, the message from these numbers is clear: If

Class of 2011

	Early	Regular	Overall
Brown	22.67%	12.27%	13.53%
Columbia	24.45	8.54	10.35
Cornell	36.56	18.94	20.70
Dartmouth	29.57	13.85	15.27
Harvard	21.83	6.40	8.97
MIT	11.17	12.77	12.32
Penn	28.87	12.43	15.95
Princeton	26.23	7.16	9.46
Stanford	16.13	8.88	10.29
Yale	19.73	6.42	9.63

ACING THE COLLEGE APPLICATION

you are aiming for a very competitive school, early is really your best chance by a long shot, sometimes almost two to one. If these numbers weren't dramatic enough, let's look at what I find to be an even more shocking comparison of how colleges now typically fill up a greater percentage of their class early than they ever did before. In the table below (using data provided in the September 2001 issue of *The Atlantic Monthly*), I've provided figures from 1991, 1996, and 2001. The number next to each college refers to the percentage of the entering freshman class that was accepted early. The number 30 means that almost one-third of the freshman

School	Percentage of Early Acceptances		
	1991	1996	2001
Amherst	23	36.7	29.8
Columbia	25	33.7	47.5
Cornell	28.7	24.3	35.8
Duke	26	33	30
Emory	19	23	36
NYU	15.5	17.1	30
Northwestern	N/A	16.8	20.7
Princeton	N/A	49.2	49.1
Stanford	N/A	34	31.5
U Penn	32.2	36.1	43
U Virginia	22	25.9	30
Yale	N/A	29	40

class was admitted early decision/early action while the remaining 70 percent were accepted by regular decision.

Let's take a moment to underline the real shockers. In 2001, Princeton filled up nearly *half* of its class early. No wonder it was nearly impossible to get accepted to Princeton by regular decision. Before they simply abolished their early program in 2006, they should have announced they were going to limit the number of early accepts to 25–30 percent of the class. It makes me angry to hear admissions people trying to tell students that they should apply early only if they are sure. That's not really true. The truth is, if you want to go to Dartmouth, you should absolutely apply early or you haven't a snowball's chance in hell of getting in under regular decision (30 percent for early decision versus 14 percent for regular). How about Columbia? They went from accepting only 25 percent to 33.7 percent to 47.5 percent. Talk about a major policy decision. I'm more impressed by colleges such as Stanford and Duke that have held the line, leaving the regular applicants a decent chance for admission.

A study done by Christopher Avery, professor at Harvard's Kennedy School of Government, and reported on in the December 24, 2001, *New York Times* backs up these findings. He and his colleagues studied more than five hundred thousand decisions at fourteen highly selective colleges from the 1990 through 1996 admissions seasons. Their main conclusion?

Applying early sharply increased some students' chance of admission. . . . On average, the ten early decision colleges accepted 70 percent of the students with SAT scores between 1400 and 1490 who applied early, but only 48 percent of those with the same scores who applied during the regular admissions process. The four early action colleges took 51 percent of the students with these scores who applied early, but only 39 percent of regular applicants with those scores.

As it turns out, there was not one category of students for whom the admittance rate was not higher than for regular applicants, often by ten to twenty percentage points.

To me, the interesting question to pose is *why* colleges are leaning toward filling a great percentage of their freshman class by early decision. Let me count the internal advantages:

1. If you fill up 40 to 50 percent of the class early, you make your life a lot easier for the rest of the year. You have to find only 50 percent rather than 80 percent of the class among thousands of applicants.

2. You establish the *exact* profile of the class in terms of SAT I scores, SAT II scores, and students with

high class ranks. For national rankings done by *U.S. News and World Report*, the academic ranking is one of the major factors determining placement. Do you think Princeton or Columbia wants to drop in SAT averages? Certainly not! How do you control those numbers? Accept lots of top kids early so you can take some riskier kids later on. In effect, you've loaded your deck with aces.

3. You make lots of alumni's children and athletes happy because these two groups are the most likely to apply early in droves.

4. As far as coaches are concerned, an athletic recruit with low academic qualification at the very least has to accept the offer. The admissions office hates nothing more than wringing its hands over a questionable athlete, only to have the athlete turn them down.

5. Any marginal candidates you accept (following the same logic as the athlete above) at least are bound to accept your offer. No need to wring hands.

6. You reward kids who are the most interested in attending your college.

None of these reasons would bother me if only the colleges were more up-front about their rationale for accepting large numbers of kids early. When a student asks, "Are my odds better if I apply early?" it seems to me an admissions officer should be duty bound to reply: "Yes, they are, and by a wide margin." Publicly discouraging applicants from rushing to apply early while at the same time filling up half the class by accepting nearly 40 percent of those who do apply early is hypocritical. Naturally, some admissions directors and college presidents are concerned. Richard Levin, the president of Yale University, made headlines when he announced to *The New York Times* on December 13, 2001, "If we all got rid of it [early decision], it would be a good thing." His comments were seen as a direct acknowledgment that elite college admissions policies were spiraling out of control. In the same article, a director of admissions elaborated, "With some of the elite schools taking higher and higher percentages of their students early decision, a growing number of kids are strategizing about where to apply, rather than looking for the place that is right for them."

No sooner did these comments appear than the presidents of two other colleges went on record saying they supported early decision. George Rupp, president of Columbia University, added, "I just don't get the argument that it is terrible and exploitative of students. . . . Without early decision, students could have to fill out six or eight applications by January." An art history professor at Columbia wrote an op-ed piece for *The New York Times* on December 18, 2001, asserting that applying for early decision takes the pressure off students: "Early decision reduces the time and money spent in applying to multiple colleges and allows some students to spend more of their senior year on something more constructive than worrying about college admission." She calls for a more streamlined process.

It would not be that difficult to overhaul the admissions process. The big problem is not early decision per se, but rather the multiple applications received by colleges during regular decision. While one college may receive fifteen thousand applications, almost all of these students are applying to between eight and ten different colleges. This means that colleges spend all their time trying to pick the best applicants only to have a lot of those applicants accept an offer from another school. If admissions directors and university presidents put their collective heads together, they could devise a system that eliminates multiple applications. Under this dream system, students would prioritize and rank their top-choice colleges. Then, they would send their application to the first college on their list. If that college accepted the student, the process would end. If they did not, the college would pass along the application to the next college on the list. Though it sounds difficult from a logistical standpoint, with computers it would not be that hard to forward documents in this way, especially if a system was designed to accommodate the details. Admissions officers would find themselves reading thousands fewer applications a year and could rest assured that if they accepted a student, the student would accept the offer. From what I understand of the "big match" system used in the medical school admissions process, a similar system is already in place for aspiring medical students. Why reinvent the wheel when admissions people could build upon this system? Students would benefit, too, because they would have to complete only one application, unlike now when students are forced to apply to ten to fifteen colleges in order to get accepted by one. After all, it's only possible to attend one college at a time.

One possible consequence of the recent elimination of early programs at a few schools is a big rise in regular applicants. If all schools dropped their early programs, for example, students would end up applying to twenty or thirty different colleges, which would overburden the system to the point of collapse. Top colleges would find themselves receiving fifty thousand applications rather than fifteen thousand (think of the cost of hiring four times the number of admissions officers to read the additional files), which would also mean even lower acceptance rates for everyone.

If colleges want to attract low-income students to apply early, they should create incentives (how about full scholarships, no loans, to all students with a family income under $100,000?), not throw out early programs altogether. Early programs are the only way for students to indicate that one college is their clear first choice.

Before closing our examination of early action and early decision, I'd like to recount a debate I had with the parent of one of my clients, who insisted that statistically speaking he thought his son had a better chance applying to several early action colleges rather than to one early decision college because the probability of admission increases as you apply to more schools. On the surface, of course, he was quite correct, but it made me think about another factor that is difficult to show or even understand through statistics alone—the difference in the quality of the early decision pool versus the early action pool.

Let's look first at a general picture of what kind of students apply early decision to competitive schools. First, you tend to get a high number of legacies (sons or daughters of graduates from that college). They are usually familiar with the college through prior family visits and ties and know that the legacy factor roughly doubles their admission rate. Why not combine the advantages of early decision with the legacy status? That's exactly what this group of students does. A few things to keep in mind: First, these applicants tend to be *lower* academically than the average admitted student. Second, there are many recruited athletes who are pressured by coaches to apply early. (As you can imagine, this group does not necessarily represent the top of the academic heap.) Third, you tend to get wealthier applicants who are less concerned with financial aid packages. After all, if you are accepted under early decision, you do not have an opportunity to compare aid packages. Finally, you get candidates who apply as long shots simply because the odds are better. Taken together, these four groups contribute to the overall lower quality of the applicant pool. Of course, there are individual exceptions, but generally, most early decision pools are much weaker than the regular applicant pool.

Let's contrast this pool of applicants with the early action pool. Typically, it is the *strongest* students in the country who apply for early action. They are fairly confident they will receive several offers of admission, so they don't feel pressured to apply for early decision. They are also interested in garnering multiple acceptances, which you can do under early action (because the decision is nonbinding, you can apply to as many schools as you like). Finally, they can compare financial aid packages from other schools.

The Avery study confirmed the difference between the early action and early decision pools. Despite certain colleges' assertions, the study proved that for the "ten colleges with early decision programs, the early decision applicants were slightly weaker, on average, than the regular admissions applicants. For the four campuses with early action programs, the early pools were somewhat stronger than the later applicants."

Given the vastly different nature of early action and early decision pools, one has to be careful in comparing raw acceptance rates at schools with different programs. It's not fair to say it's easier to get into school X, which accepts 30 percent by early decision, than it is to get into school Y, which accepts 35 percent by early action. Those numbers may be closer than you think because it is likely that the latter's applicant pool is much stronger overall. It's interesting to note that colleges are slowly realizing that even though early action is great for the candidate, it's not particularly advantageous to the admissions office. As I noted earlier, with early decision the college can control the exact demographic of the freshman class. With early action, except for a school such as Harvard, which has an extraordinarily high early action yield (the number of students who say yes to the offer), colleges find it hard to predict how many of the accepted students will attend.

I'd like to end this chapter by making a statistical observation based on Ivy League data, although from the numbers I've seen, most of the less selective colleges mirror the proportions. Between 15 and 20 percent of the freshman class at the Ivies are recruited athletes; roughly 10 to 15 percent are black, Hispanic, or Native American; roughly 4 to 8 percent are legacies; and roughly 1 to 3 percent are development/VIP students (either potential big donors or famous people). Taken together, on average at the Ivies a full 40 percent of the freshman class is basically reserved for special cases (minorities, athletes, legacies, development cases, and VIPs). That means that for a normal nontargeted applicant, the odds are even worse than the acceptance rate you see printed in *U.S. News and World Report*. For example, if the overall acceptance rate is 20 percent, the nontagged applicant is aiming for the 60 percent of space left in the class, making the actual acceptance rate closer to 15 percent. Despite colleges' well-intentioned pleas to avoid making a rash early action or early decision choice, students would do well to weigh their advice very carefully given the much higher admit rate at most colleges under early decision. While early action may not make a big difference, early decision definitely does. Anyone who tries to minimize the hard numbers is misleading you. Considering that you may be aiming for the 60 percent of available space left in a class, the early decision versus regular decision may be the most important choice you make in terms of maximizing your chances at the college of your choice. Take advantage of early programs before too many colleges follow Harvard and Princeton's lead in abolishing them.

14

EXTRA MATERIALS—
WHAT TO SEND AND
WHAT NOT TO SEND

 ## THE GOOD, THE BAD, AND THE UGLY

There are admissions-related urban legends about the various desperate moves students have resorted to in order to further their applications—everything from a gigantic fresh salmon from a Canadian student to a ten-foot smiley-faced cookie baked by another applicant. My advice? Do not send *anything* to the admissions office besides your application materials. Any gimmick you use will work against you. However, there are a few things you can and should send, so let's break these down by category. Note that the new Common Application includes an art supplement, an athletic supplement, and an international supplement, so for the first time, you can use these forms with your materials.

Sports

Athletic recruiting is a separate process that happens along-side the admissions process. Basically, coaches recruit and make lists of the students they'd like to have and pass these lists along to the admissions office (who at that point usually cross off many of the coaches' less-strong academic choices). If you are a viable Division I, Division II, or Division III re-cruit and you come from a nonestablished program, feel free to e-mail the athletic offices at the colleges you are interested in. They will take it from there, asking you to submit forms, grades, whatever they need. If the coaches ask you for a video, send one to *them*. At all costs avoid sending anything directly to the admissions office, because the coaches handle this process. The last thing the admissions office wants to do is watch your football tape. Don't be shy about establishing a preliminary contact with the appropriate coach (e-mail makes this easy, because most colleges list their coaches' addresses right on the school's Web page). They will then request the necessary information.

Music

Again, do not send in a tape directly to the admissions office unless they specifically direct you to do so in their applica-tion directions. It's not unusual for admissions offices to col-lect all the tapes sent in by students and then have a party (sometimes with substantial amounts of alcohol) at which they watch them all for bawdy entertainment. You do *not* want your video to reach this unenviable end. The admissions office is not the correct body to evaluate your musical talent—for admissions purposes, you should list your awards (All-State, any competitions you have won) and they will believe you. If you say you're an All-State clarinet player, they trust that you are quite good.

Go the extra mile—if you're really a talented musician and have a few colleges you're very interested in, contact them as early as your junior year (again by e-mail), briefly addressing your musical talents and your desire to attend that college. Ask if they'd like you to come up and play for them or send a tape. If they say yes, do so. At that point, if the music department decides they are dying for a clarinet player for the symphony orchestra, they will follow up by sending a note to the admissions office, assigning you a rank. This constitutes an admissions flag—flags help a student stand out from the pack. In other words, contact the music department directly, determine who the appropriate person is (orchestra conductor, or leader of the jazz group), and find out where to go from there. If they are impressed by you, write them a note affirming your interest in the school and ask them to pass along a note to the admissions office. (They should know how to do this, but you're just reminding them that you are very interested in their school.)

Art/Photography

No surprise here—the admissions office cannot judge the artistic merit of your photos, paintings, or ink drawings. Therefore, it is totally pointless to send a portfolio to the admissions office. Once again, the admissions office will believe you if you discuss your artistic talent and list your awards. If you want your talent to help you get in and you intend to pursue this talent in college, contact the art department. They might request a portfolio, in which case you should prepare one and send it. Always follow up and ask if they've sent their evaluation of your work to the admissions office.

Extra Letters of Recommendation

This is one area where students go overboard. Keep in mind that less is more. If you send in too many extra letters, it will indicate to the admissions office a lack of confidence in your application. After all, why do you need that many letters saying you're great when your talents should come across in the application? The key is moderation. Yes, you can send in *one* extra letter if it relates to an activity that has taken a huge amount of time. For instance, if you've spent hours doing research in a lab and have discussed your research in your application, by all means have the head researcher write a letter on your behalf. What you don't really need is a letter from your clergyman saying what a nice kid you are. Colleges assume you are nice, so why send extra stuff, which will only clog up your file? The other mistake students make is having famous people who don't really know them write a letter. Let me state clearly that having Bill Clinton write a letter saying what a nice guy (or girl) you are and how he worked with your parents is *not* going to help you get into college. If you are truly a development case, your application will be marked as such, but it's not these silly letters that do that, it's the development office, an entire office devoted to fund-raising and making lists of major donors and influential members of the board. So when your parents tell you that Senator X, who is a friend of your father's partner, wants to write a letter for you because he went to Yale, just say no thanks—it hurts more often than it helps. Let your achievements stand for themselves. As far as teacher recommendations, if you really have another teacher (beyond the two required) who you feel can add something meaningful to your academic profile, you can submit one extra letter, but that's it. You do *not* want to bog down your application with multiple letters.

Papers and Projects

I can recall hundreds of students every year sending in their term papers, science projects, literary essays, poetry collections, et cetera. Remember, the admissions committee is not made up of professors. Unless a college specifically requests a research paper, do *not* send any supplementary materials. If you want a visual, picture this: The weary admissions officer reaches into the drawer of files to pull out his daily quota of thirty that he then has to lug back to his house to read. He looks with horror on one fat file that has a thirty-page paper wedged in it. He glances around, hopes no one else is watching, and sticks that one in the back so he doesn't have to carry it. Get the picture? No one wants to read your paper. If it's a strong paper, contact the appropriate department, make contact with a professor in that field, and ask if you can send it to her. A professor's letter of recommendation carries a great deal of weight, so it's an excellent idea to initiate contact with a professor, but do *not* send it to the admissions office.

Newspapers, Magazines, et Cetera

By now I'll assume that you're following this discussion carefully and you can predict the answer—do *not* send in your award-winning newspaper or magazine even if you produced the whole thing and wrote every article. You can describe your work in the application, list the awards you have won, but there is no need to send in an example. They will believe you.

Summary

Be very careful not to impose upon an already heavily burdened admissions office. If you send in any extra materials to the admissions office, be sure they're short. The staff may take the time to read one poem or a short essay or a magazine article, but the last thing they want to do is read your science paper. Feel free to describe the research you did, but don't include the project itself. The general rule is that it's always good to establish contact with specific departments in the college—often they will request that you send them the additional materials. All you want the admissions office to end up with is a letter from that college department saying that they'd love to have you play clarinet for them or that they were blown away by your research paper. Let the experts in their respective fields judge you. Do not expect the admissions office to be made up of those experts. The bottom line is, be considerate of their time and effort to get through literally thousands of applications in a short application season. Don't make their job harder than it already is. Talk about your accomplishments, but do not feel like you have to support them with lengthy examples or supplemental materials.

15
ETHICAL DILEMMAS AND EXPLANATORY NOTES

There are some well-circulated stories of students who were rejected due to ethical violations, most notably the Harvard admit who murdered her mother and was subsequently unaccepted. Most ethical dilemmas occur on a smaller scale—an incident of plagiarism, cheating, or drinking. What should students do in the case of a known violation?

Often students are unsure as to whether an incident will be mentioned by the school. Increasingly, high schools worry about legal issues and are reluctant to disclose incidents or mention them on a student's official record. I've worked in several private schools where incidents are hushed up so they don't hurt a student's chances for admission.

The main problem is that the student will seldom know whether the school has mentioned the incident or not. After all, colleges receive two letters of recommendation and a guidance counselor letter from the school; there's plenty of opportunity for someone to mention an incident. As I mentioned earlier, now that the new version of the Common Application specifically asks students and the guidance counselor about infractions, you simply have to assume it will be mentioned.

Again, my advice is to be honest. It is much better to acknowledge an incident than to ignore it completely, especially in the case where a school official mentions it. In that case, it would look as though you were avoiding the problem or trying to cover it up. Because you can never be 100 percent sure what the school will and won't mention, it's better to err on the side of explaining the incident.

Colleges treat infractions on a case-by-case basis. Some incidents that might have seemed troubling to a high school may be of less concern to a college. I remember one example from Dartmouth of a private school student who got caught having a glass of wine with another student's parents at a local restaurant. They were celebrating a grandparent's birthday and the parents poured wine for the students. Unfortunately, a faculty member was present and reported the incident because that school had a zero tolerance policy for alcohol. Though the school did not mention it, the student was very forthright and wrote a short note explaining the circumstances of his suspension. Because he was honest and because the infraction was not considered very serious from our standpoint, the whole incident was discounted.

However, certain incidents, particularly those concerning

academic dishonesty such as cheating or plagiarism, are considered grave offenses. For colleges, their currency is intellectual thought. Notice how on the recent MIT scandal, the director of admissions had to resign immediately when it was discovered she had lied about where she had attended college. Thus it is the equivalent of grand larceny or theft to steal someone else's ideas through either plagiarism or another form of cheating. Students should keep this in mind as they progress through high school—cheating of any kind is not worth the risk. Far better to fail on your own than to pass with illegal help.

The lapse will be explained in the context of the student's record. For example, an incident that took place in ninth grade would not be as serious as one that took place junior year. You owe it to the admissions office to explain the circumstances, the infraction, and the punishment, but more important, tell them what lessons you learned from the incident. Remember, colleges are institutions of higher learning and as such are concerned with students' ability to learn from their mistakes. College admissions officers are not perfect themselves—almost anyone can hark back to childhood mischief that could cause embarrassment if it were to surface.

That is why I advocate for full disclosure and honesty on the students' part. Students must present their side of the story, especially if the details are disputed. I can think of one student who recorded that he had been charged with assaulting another student at his school and suspended for two days. It turned out that the school overreacted a little to the incident. In actual fact (we called the school to confirm the student's story), another student had punched this student's friend in the face. After he saw that his friend was getting pummeled, he pounced on the attacker and pulled him off, ripping his shirt in the process. As luck would have it, the witnessing teacher saw only that part, not the first scuffle, and reported an assault. Once we heard the student's side of the story, it was clear that the incident was not as grave as it first seemed.

Colleges are concerned about behavioral incidents because many have strong honor codes—the last thing they want on their campus is a student prone to cheating. Likewise, they do not want to endanger the lives of other students by admitting a volatile student who is prone to violent behavior. That is why colleges ask both students and guidance counselors to disclose any incidents. Many are afraid to do so, but I can assure you that it is much worse not to disclose an incident than to take the chance to explain the surrounding circumstances.

Other Notes

Often students wish they had the chance to explain something directly to an admissions officer. Perhaps the school's block scheduling has prevented a student from taking five difficult classes because of scheduling conflicts, or perhaps a low grade could be explained by a death in the family or a health incident. In any case where further explanation is needed, students should feel free to add an extra page to the application entitled something to the effect of "please note." For example: "Please note that my course load looks lighter than it should because our school allows only four block courses to be taken at a time. I was not able to take both AP English and AP Studio Art because of a scheduling conflict. Thank you for your understanding."

Students make the mistake of counting on their high school to point out this type of thing, but that is often not a good idea. Never assume that anyone will add any information on your behalf. If you want to be sure something is mentioned, write a note and add it to your application. Here's one more example: "You may notice when evaluating my high school transcript that I failed biology freshman year. Though I am not trying to make excuses, ten of the twelve students failed the class because we had five different teachers over the course of the year. My school would not change the grades, so many of us were stuck with an unacceptably low grade." In the preceding example, it is very helpful to know the full situation. Of course, an admissions person would be surprised by an anomalous low grade, but an explanation like this is useful in dispelling doubts about the student's ability.

If there is anything at all, either personal or academic, that has affected your performance in high school, take a moment to provide a brief explanation. No need to write a lengthy treatise—a short explanatory note will do the trick. Admissions officers will appreciate the clarification. You may be addressing the very issue they have identified as problematic in your application.

16

WHAT TO DO IF YOU ARE DEFERRED OR WAIT-LISTED

There are three possibilities for early decision or early action candidates: accepted, rejected, or deferred. To borrow from Dante, if getting accepted is Paradiso and getting rejected is Inferno, then getting deferred qualifies as Purgatorio— somewhere between heaven and hell. For those who apply under regular decision, you can be accepted, rejected, or put on the wait list. Like getting deferred, being wait-listed puts you in the unusual circumstance of being in limbo. Nothing is more depressing than to be rejected, deferred, or wait-listed by your first-choice college. If you are rejected, there is nothing you can do, but if you are deferred or wait-listed, there are some steps you can take to improve your chances of getting in.

Deferrals and Wait Lists

Students usually find out in mid-December that they have been deferred. Typically, they get upset or depressed and sit around during winter break wondering what led to the deferral. Although all the deferral letters look the same, there are several types of deferrals, none of which would be obvious to the applicant. Some students are deferred because they were missing information: test scores, recent grades, a teacher recommendation, or something else. There is usually not enough time to call applicants to ask them for this missing information, so the admissions offices respond by deferring. Assuming that the missing information is very positive, this would be a valid deferral and a somewhat encouraging one. Next comes the polite deferral—someone in the admissions office realizes they will never admit a student (not interesting enough, not enough passion or initiative) but the applicant is too strong to reject outright. Often special category students—legacies, recruited athletes, minorities—will be given a polite deferral. After all, it is much more politic to defer an alumni's son or daughter than to reject him or her and then have to deal with an angry parent. Sometimes admissions offices even respond to guidance counselor requests to defer rather than reject a student to take some of the pressure off the counselor, who might be blamed.

How can you, the student, get a sense about what kind of deferral yours was? The only way is to call right after you get your deferral letter and ask to speak to the admissions officer in charge of reading your application. Because all admissions officers will be out of the office during Christmas/winter break, it behooves you to call very soon after receiving the letter. Take a day off from school if you have to and call the admissions office. Usually, you will get a secretary or receptionist. Tell that person your name and region and ask if you can get a return phone call about your application. You will rarely be sent directly to an admissions officer because no one will want to speak to you without first reviewing your folder. Your initial phone call triggers the secretary to pull your materials and place them in the hands of the admissions officer, who will read over the notes on your file and return your call. Believe it or not, very few students have the courage to call—more often than not, students let their parents call or don't bother. Therefore, admissions officers have a great deal of respect for the student mature enough to call in person to find out additional information. You should know that most offices document these kinds of calls and add a note to the file. The admissions officer would write something like, "Alex Smith called on 12/16 to discuss his deferral. I told him that we never received his SAT II Math IIC scores, which turned out to be an error on the College Board's part. In addition to sending the official scores (he got a 740), Alex mentioned that he was nominated at his school for a big state award for leadership. Let's keep an eye on him." Colleges notice that the student was courageous enough to call in person.

When you receive a return call from the admissions office,

be courteous and positive—of course, you are disappointed by your deferral, but you are calling to find out if there were any specific shortcomings or areas the admissions officer feels you should concentrate on. Basically, you are asking for any information that would be helpful both to this application and to any future ones you will send out for regular decision.

There are many possible reasons for deferrals, some of which would be too confidential to share with the applicant, so it's important for you to listen between the lines. If the admissions officer keeps repeating how hard it was to get in early and how few were accepted without offering any concrete information, you should understand that there truly is not much you can do. Perhaps there was some confidential information (a teacher saying that you were a grade-grubber who didn't love learning or were just not a standout at your school, an incident of academic dishonesty from ninth grade, or anything else) that an admissions office is not permitted to share with you for legal or confidentiality reasons.

However, if you learn that your file was incomplete, your test scores were never received, or you didn't elaborate enough on your activities, there are steps you can take to improve your chances. Many times the admissions office will defer strong candidates because they want to see one more set of senior grades to make sure that student is receiving good grades in senior year. Especially for students who may have gotten off to a slow start in high school, an upwardly mobile grade trend is critical. If this is the case, you know your primary job is to do your very best to get the highest grades possible for the rest of the year and to have your guidance counselor submit a positive midyear report.

If you want to cover all your bases, you should call the admissions office yourself and then request that your guidance counselor do the same. The purpose of the counselor's call is really twofold: first, to find out more specific reasons about your deferral (admissions officers can be very candid with guidance counselors), and second, to advocate for you and update the admissions office quickly on any other accomplishments you may have. Conscientious guidance counselors will do this without prompting, but it's always good to request the favor. I had guidance counselors call to tell me we'd really made a big mistake and that so-and-so was really the most highly regarded student at the school, a leader, and a super student. It certainly is possible to make mistakes in the pressure-cooker atmosphere of trying to read thousands of folders in a short period, so a personal update from the guidance counselor can definitely help. Again, the admissions person would take notes on the phone call and update the file accordingly.

Once you and your guidance counselor have met and discussed the findings, you have to decide upon a next step. If your counselor tells you there is little hope, odds are the admissions officer probably shared some confidential information with the counselor about why you were not admitted. In this case, move on. However, if your sense is that there is hope, jump into action.

Over winter break, be sure to devote time to your other applications before you do anything else. At most colleges, only 5 to 10 percent of those candidates who are deferred are ultimately accepted, so the odds are not in your favor. For this reason, it makes sense to be as thorough as you can by completing your other applications on time for the January 1 or 15 deadlines. Besides, once you have communicated directly with the admissions officer, there is little else you can do before vacation.

Now timing becomes important. Let's look at things from the admissions office's point of view. Admissions officers were on the road in September, October, and November recruiting students and visiting schools. With hardly time to catch their breath, they moved right into early decision and began reading applications five to eight hours a day. With early decision, they don't start reading until about November 15 or so and have to be done with all the files by around December 5 in order to make final decisions and mail the letters out by December 10. Then they have to field why-did-you-defer-me phone calls for a week and suddenly it's Christmas break. Exhausted, they try to escape the drudgery of admissions reading for a few brief weeks, and then in January they are confronted with the real reading season with thousands more applications to read every day from January to March.

I'm sure it's obvious now why you should not bombard the admissions office with phone calls, e-mails, or any other communications during January or February—they are busy. Most are at home reading twenty-five to thirty applications a day, sometimes as much as eight hours at a time. Their focus is simply on getting through multiple readings of thousands of applicants before March. Once that job is finally under control, all admissions offices devote one or two days in mid-March or so to revisiting the deferred applicants. Like everything else in admissions, the task is a bit overwhelming and they try to get it over with as quickly as possible. Sometime during this March window, all the deferred applicants are brought back to the regional officers in charge of those areas. That person is in charge of reading through as many as a hundred files and rifling through any new information that would be right in the front of the folder. You do not want to send too much material because it will never be looked at. However, sometime before March 1 you should write a brief letter reaffirming your interest in that school (if it's still your first choice, be sure to say so), and then attach a brief summary of any new information in list form. If necessary, split the page into an academic section and an extracurricular section. It's okay to be brief and to the point. Let's look at an example of an updated list.

- Retook the SAT IIs in January: scored 680 on writing and 700 on chemistry.
- Received five A's and one A-minus in my six-AP course load, the highest of anyone in my class.

- Finished a major research project for the National Science Foundation on enzyme production in lab rats, which will be published in March.

- After a contentious board meeting, was elected editor in chief of our 150-year-old daily newspaper, a major time commitment.

- In track, won my division in the high jump competition and was nominated captain.

In a nutshell, the admissions officer can get a quick idea of the improvements to the student's original application. Of course, it still matters why the student was deferred in the first place. In the best case, if this student had been deferred because the admissions staffer was worried that grades would decline, this student would have a decent chance because the course load is unusually rigorous and the grades spectacular. Plus, this student kept pushing for leadership positions while excelling in sports, research, and general activities. There is no evidence of senior slump in this update. It was brief enough to detain the admissions person for only five minutes or less, but long enough to detail the specific accomplishments. Along with a brief note that this college is still the student's first choice, this student would have done the appropriate amount of work to show that there was no falloff in performance.

If you originally had either an e-mail or a personal contact with your regional admissions officers, mid-March would also be an appropriate time to either call or e-mail your admissions officer to reaffirm your interest and to draw his attention to your most recent achievements. Why so much contact? Clearly, if the admissions officer is mandated to select a small percentage of applicants from the deferred pile, the applicant with the most personal connection who clearly demonstrates his desire to attend is going to get picked over another candidate who never even bothered to call, write, or send an update. Though the odds are still not in the deferred candidate's favor, those odds are dramatically increased if appropriate steps are taken at the right time.

The wait list functions the same way except you want to make even more of a nuisance of yourself. Like the deferral tips, you want to send an update, reaffirm your interest, establish personal contact by phone or e-mail, and make sure that the admissions officer knows your name. If your guidance counselor can help by advocating for you, all the better. Sometimes luck will be against you on the wait list—when colleges place students on the wait list, they have no idea if they will accept one or one hundred students from the list. If it happens that year that the yield is very high, they may never get to the wait list. But if they are able to select some students, they will undoubtedly pick the ones they have a personal interest in, ones that they have spoken to and know are dying to attend that school. Admissions officers hate debating whether to admit a student from the wait list only to find out the student is no longer interested. It is definitely worth your while to reaffirm your interest and to represent any significant accomplishments. Resist the temptation to do anything gimmicky like parking your old Volkswagen bus, painted with school colors, outside the admissions office. These types of things will only take away from your chances. Stick to your own firm accomplishments.

Though policy varies from office to office, most admissions directors allow their regional people one or more freebie picks who would otherwise be rejected. Your goal should be to make yourself known to the admissions person so that you are the first prospect to come to mind. You have nothing to lose—if your achievements are not sufficient, you won't be admitted anyway, but your goal is to tilt the odds in your favor by maximizing your chances of admission.

Summary

1. Don't give up if you are deferred or wait-listed.
2. Do call the admissions officer personally to find out as much as you can.
3. Do have your guidance counselor call to put in a good word for you and to find out any additional information.
4. Do speak with your counselor to compare notes.
5. Make it a priority to finish your other applications over winter break so that you don't jeopardize your chances at other colleges by being late.

6. If your testing is questionable, do sign up right away to take the January SAT I or SAT II because admissions officers may be waiting for improved scores.

7. Do study extra hard and have your best academic year ever.

8. Do devote time to figuring out how to keep up your momentum as far as prizes, awards, and achievements are concerned—you want to show improvement in as many areas as possible.

9. Do not call the admissions office or send in tons of extra material in January or February.

10. Do use the first week in March to prepare a brief cover letter and update to send to the admissions office. You may want to reiterate why that college is still your first choice.

11. Do follow up by e-mailing or calling your admissions person to make personal contact and to draw his or her attention to your application and new accomplishments.

12. Don't flood your file with extraneous recommendations, music tapes, videos, long papers, or anything else that would clutter your folder. Keep it simple and direct.

13. Don't give up until it's over. Keep pushing until you hear one way or the other.

14. If you are accepted, follow up with a personal phone call to thank the admissions person who advocated for you. A little appreciation goes a long way.

15. Do remember to respond right away and to accept the offer of admission. Do send in a deposit to secure your place.

17

WEIGHING YOUR OPTIONS ONCE YOU'RE ACCEPTED

Naturally, if you are accepted early decision you have no options to weigh because you are bound to attend that college. The only exception would be if for some reason the financial aid package proved totally unacceptable. This is extremely rare because colleges understand that students who apply early decision effectively give up their right to compare packages, so they are very sure to be fair. Plus, if you found your package unsatisfactory, you first have to appeal it directly by speaking to the financial aid office. I can almost guarantee that if they will not budge an inch, you stand almost no chance of getting a better package at another school. Once the college has accepted you, it is in their best interest to do whatever they can to help. I would always try to avoid wiggling out of an early decision agreement, colleges take that commitment very seriously. If you use the process as a game, no one will be amused—it could even have adverse consequences for you in applications to other schools if word spreads that you got out of a binding agreement. Why would you want to put yourself in that position?

Moving on to early action, if you are accepted to one or more colleges, consider it a major feather in your cap. Because you'll hear well before the January 1 deadline, take stock of your complete list of colleges. If you've been accepted to a competitive college, now there is no need to apply to less competitive colleges as safety schools. Likewise, eliminate any colleges (even if they are more competitive) that you are no longer interested in. One of my greatest complaints about the college admissions process is that too many students apply to too many schools, thereby clogging the admissions pipelines. Be grateful that you have some early options (most students won't) and eliminate all but your very top-choice colleges for the regular round. To put it another way, the only colleges still on your list should be those you would definitely attend instead of the ones to which you have already been accepted.

Let's fast-forward to February/March. For the most part, you will be playing the waiting game, but be aware that some colleges do send out what they call likely letters to top candidates. They send these well in advance of the final decisions, which are not mailed out until April. If you are lucky enough to receive one, it will read something like, "Although at this time we are not allowed to issue a formal acceptance letter, it is likely that when we do send those letters out in April, you will be accepted." You'd think this is pretty self-explanatory, but parents and students usually panic and call the admissions office to ask what this means. My feeling is that if you call in to ask, you should be taken off the likely list.

I guess the problem is that it sounds too good to be true, but increasingly colleges are using these letters as a way to increase their yield. From the student's point of view, won't he be more likely to favor the school that gives him the courtesy of letting him know early rather than the school that waits? I know if I were applying to Yale and Dartmouth, I'd be more likely to attend the one that sent me a likely letter. The problem is that very few students get them because of the sheer quantity of applications colleges receive. To receive a likely letter, you not only have to be in the very top of the applicant pool, you also have to have the blind luck to have been read by enough admissions counselors by a certain date. Those two processes don't come together very often, so don't expect a likely letter, but if you do get one, think of it as a nice option for you. Yes, a likely letter is just like an admit letter and you will definitely be accepted, barring any criminal behavior or huge drop in academic performance.

Finally, let's fast-forward to April. If you didn't apply under any early options and you have not received any likely letters, you should hear from all the schools you applied to no later than April 10. If for some reason you have not heard from a particular school, give them a call and ask for the decision over the phone. After a certain date, offices will release decisions on the phone to the student who provides proper ID (Social Security number and birthday). By April 10, you will most likely have some acceptance letters, some rejection letters, and maybe one or two wait-list letters. This is the time to make your decision. Usually, the acceptance letters arrive at the beginning of April—it's good to remember that the common reply date is not until May 1. There is *no* advantage in accepting an offer early so you might as well make a thoughtful decision.

If there is any doubt at all about which school to accept, take the three to four weeks and visit one or more campuses. Most students don't realize that colleges set up special programs for accepted students and will even pay for less well-off students to fly to their campuses during this time. Even if you have to pay, isn't it worth the money or the trip to make one more visit so you can get a feel for the campus? After all, you'll be spending the next four years of your life at that campus. Colleges will usually pair you up with another student during your visit so be sure to ask lots of questions, attend a class or two, eat at a dining hall, and participate in as many activities as you can while you are there.

Some students express concern that they can't afford to miss classes at their high school. At this point in time, don't worry too much about your high school classes. Sure, if your grades drop dramatically, colleges do reserve the right to reject you once you've been accepted, but we are talking about an A average dropping to a C or two or more classes with D or F grades. Even one C won't finish you off because most colleges allow for one C, especially in calculus. I can't emphasize what an important decision you have before you: Take the time to visit campuses even if you have done so before. Unlike during your previous visit, chances are that this time classes will be in session so you will have a more accurate idea of what life is like on campus.

Once you have done additional homework on the colleges (perhaps looking up your areas of interest in the course catalog to see which of the colleges has a better selection) and made additional visits, you are ready to decide. Which college is your true first choice? If you were accepted by early action, do any of your regular acceptances look more attractive? Your final step is to list your order of preference. If you did not apply for financial aid, you are now finished. Send in your acceptance along with a deposit or whatever the school requests.

If you did apply for financial aid, compare financial aid awards at your top-choice schools. What should you do if your second-choice school has a more attractive aid package than your first-choice school? Now is the time to call the financial aid office at your first-choice school and fax them the other school's award letter. Once you are accepted, they will review your information and compare it to your other package. Keep in mind that colleges will make changes only for colleges they see as comparable to their own. For example, Harvard will not increase your aid package just because your local community college or perhaps your state school offered you more money. In effect, those other schools are offering you merit money. Very few of the top colleges give merit awards—most awards are based solely on financial need. But, if you were accepted to both Yale and Harvard but wanted to go to Yale, the odds are good that Yale would add more money to your package.

Be flexible—remember that colleges can shift things around to make them more attractive without adding more dollars. Between two equal monetary awards, it's preferable to have fewer loans and a higher grant amount. Some colleges, such as Princeton, have done away with loans entirely. It's to your benefit to minimize your loans and maximize your grant money. In short, two academically similar colleges will often allow you to appeal a financial aid package, but two very different colleges will not award you any further money.

Like most things in life, you'll never know unless you ask. Colleges care very much about their yield and will do everything within their power to convince accepted students to take them up on their admission offer.

A final note about the wait list—what do you do if you have an acceptable choice but your top-choice college has placed you on the wait list? The first order of business is to secure your place at the first college so you don't lose the offer. Send in the deposit and accept the offer. In the worst case, you'll be taken off the wait list, accept another offer, and lose your deposit. Then, you need to turn your attention to the wait list school. First, fill in the card they send you saying that you'd like to be placed on the official wait list. Those who don't respond are not really "on" the wait list anymore. Once you are wait-listed, there are several ways you can still pursue your candidacy. If you happen to have already been accepted to comparable schools, you may want to call personally and speak to an admissions officer directly about your chances. Basically, you want to establish a personal contact with someone who realizes that you were accepted to Georgetown, Northwestern, Duke, and Brown but your first choice is still Penn. Chances are that Penn might accept you because in effect they are stealing you away from some very good colleges. They might even question themselves for not accepting you in the first place.

I know that at Dartmouth, we would often take kids off the wait list if we knew they were accepted to our rival schools (Yale, Harvard, Princeton, Brown, and Georgetown) but preferred our school. Use that information to your advantage. Sometimes the reverse is true—it's not inconceivable that you would be accepted into several top colleges but then rejected by some slightly less competitive colleges. Sometimes this latter group might have thought you looked too strong for their pool and assumed you were applying only as a backup. I can almost guarantee that if you were accepted to Harvard but rejected at Tufts, that's what happened. If you really wanted to attend Tufts, just fax them your Harvard acceptance and then tell them why you'd rather attend Tufts.

As you can see, to have any chance on the wait list, you will have to be persistent—make follow-up phone calls and e-mails, send additional information, and check back every few weeks. This is how the admissions office knows you are still interested. Don't be discouraged if the process drags on until June or July. Remember, they won't know until a few weeks after May 1 exactly how many students have accepted their offers of admission. Then, they have to appeal financial aid, offer a few extensions (yes, you can get an extension if you need an extra week to plan a visit), wait for late mail, and tabulate the results carefully before deciding how many applicants (if any) they will take off the wait list. At that point in time, they are going to take those students who are the strongest academically and who have expressed the greatest interest in attending their school.

If you are accepted off the wait list, wait until you have the written offer before calling back your other college and withdrawing your acceptance. Be aware that you will lose your deposit. Don't worry about offending the college— every college loses a few kids every year, so they build that number into their tallies. They even account for summer attrition—every year there are a few students who opt to take a year off or get off the wait list late in the game.

Although the last thing you will want to do at this point is focus on your school work, keep in mind a few details:

1. Do *not* let your grades slip. Sure, you can get a B here and there, but remember that all admittances are conditional (read your acceptance letter closely)—you still have to finish the year in style.

2. Do *not* get into any major disciplinary trouble. Colleges can still reject you in the case of a major incident at their discretion. Be especially aware of academic honesty violations—these are taboo in academic environments. If you have to resort to cheating, you don't deserve to attend your first-choice college.

3. Do *not* blow off your AP or IB exams. Though the admissions committee won't see your scores, you can get a *lot* of college credit if you do well. I saved a whole term's worth of tuition at Dartmouth (ten thousand dollars) by spending a few hundred dollars on AP tests. That's a good return on your investment. Besides the financial incentive, even lower scores will often exempt you from lower level classes. If you are thinking of being premed, you'll want to be exempt from as many of the hypercompetitive premed courses as you can.

4. Have the courtesy to send thank-you notes to all the schools that accepted you. Be sure to say where you are attending. Remember—at this point, you never know what will happen. Conceivably you may decide to transfer the following year if it turns out you're not happy where you are, so don't burn your bridges. Admissions offices will file your correspondence right in your original application folder.

5. Relax—you survived one of the most difficult processes you will have to face in life. Now that you've been accepted, read some books for fun, have dinner with your friends, go see those movies you've been waiting for—all this is part of getting ready for college.

ACKNOWLEDGMENTS

First and foremost I would like to thank my incredible parents and my sister, Jennifer, who not only provided emotional support and endless doses of humor for years but even volunteered to read through an early manuscript, a laborious task. My aunt and uncle, Susan and Ralph, were also helpful in sending relevant articles, researching some points, and providing a handy guinea pig with my cousin, Michael, who is now all grown up.

Hats off to my incredible students and their families from the past eight years who were a pleasure to work with and who gamely granted permission for me to use their original works in this book—they all know who they are.

I would also like to thank Sandra Abt, who took all my frantic calls during both the writing of this book and my doctoral dissertation and kept me on the straight and narrow path of academic scholarship. I also want to thank Ballantine associate managing editor Nancy Delia, and Sue Warga, my copyeditor. Heartfelt love and thanks to my circle of friends, who give me the best reason in the world for rising each day to face the tasks at hand (and who repeatedly told me I was crazy to take on a book project while writing a dissertation, doing course work, and running a business—as usual, they were right): Tracy, Jeanne, Margo and Andrew, Jana, Julie and Nathan, Laura, Sue and Pete, Sheila, Cristine, and Yvonne (fellow stargazer to boot). I am eternally grateful for such a close-knit group of loyal and longtime friends who continued to support me during the months it took to completely revise and update this book.

There are many people to thank in the publishing world: my fantastic agent, Robin Straus, who always knows exactly what to do in every situation (and whose unblinking critical eye allowed me to see my work in an objective light); her husband, Joseph Kanon, whose books kept me entertained during my few breaks from writing; and my terrific and supportive editors at Ballantine, Elisabeth Kallick Dyssegaard and Christina Duffy.

Thanks to my beautiful daughter, Alexia, who patiently endured my grueling work schedule, and to Bruce, my loving husband. Of course, with the arrival of my son, Ian James, I have to thank him for being the most adorable baby boy on the planet. I would hate to leave out my two gorgeous golden retrievers, Harris and Bree, who can typically be found curled up under my desk at my feet as I write.

Michele A. Hernández, Ed.D., has come to be known as the "admissions guru" through her college consulting work with high school students and her books *Acing the College Application, A Is for Admission,* and *The Middle School Years.* Hernández is one of America's leading experts in selective college admissions and counseling services and has been featured in hundreds of newspapers, magazines, and radio and television programs, including *Newsweek, Bloomberg, The New York Times, The Wall Street Journal, The New York Post, The Atlantic Monthly, The Today Show,* CNN, and MSNBC.

As an assistant director of admissions at Dartmouth College for four years and the academic dean of a private high school in South Florida, Hernández has crafted a unique angle for assisting students in gaining admission to the most selective colleges, incorporating her "inside perspective" on the admissions adventure. Dr. Hernández graduated Phi Beta Kappa from Dartmouth College in 1989 and went on to earn a master's degree in English and comparative literature from Columbia University and a doctorate in education. She and her family live in Weybridge, Vermont.

Portland Community College